NEX FAITH

MW00576363

12
SPIRITUAL
PRACTICES
FOR YOUTH

JEFF GRENELL

WHITAKER
HOUSE

Note: This book is not intended to provide medical advice or to take the place of medical advice and treatment from your personal physician. Neither the publisher nor the author takes any responsibility for any possible consequences from any action taken by any person reading or following the information in this book. Always consult your physician or other qualified health care professional before undertaking any change in your physical regimen, whether fasting, diet, medications, or exercise.

Unless otherwise indicated, all Scripture quotations are taken from *The Holy Bible, English Standard Version,* © 2016, 2001, 2000, 1995 by Crossway Bibles, a division of Good News Publishers. Used by permission. All rights reserved. Scripture quotations marked (NIV) are taken from the *Holy Bible, New International Version*®, NIV®, © 1973, 1978, 1984, 2011 by Biblica, Inc.® Used by permission of Zondervan. All rights reserved worldwide. www.zondervan.com. The "NIV" and "New International Version" are trademarks registered in the United States Patent and Trademark Office by Biblica, Inc.® Scripture quotations marked (AMP) are taken from *The Amplified® Bible,* © 2015 by The Lockman Foundation, La Habra, CA. Used by permission. (www.Lockman.org). All rights reserved. Scripture quotations marked (NKJV) are taken from the *New King James Version,* © 1982 by Thomas Nelson, Inc. Used by permission. All rights reserved. Scripture quotations marked (MSG) are taken from *The Message: The Bible in Contemporary Language* by Eugene H. Peterson, © 1993, 2002, 2018. Used by permission of NavPress Publishing Group. All rights reserved. Represented by Tyndale House Publishers, Inc.

NEXT GEN FAITH
12 Spiritual Practices for Youth

www.ythology.com
511 South 4th St. #608
Minneapolis, MN 55415
616.638.6854
jeffgrenell@ythology.com

ISBN: 978-1-64123-922-6
eBook ISBN: 978-1-64123-923-3
Printed in Colombia

© 2023 by Jeff Grenell

Whitaker House
1030 Hunt Valley Circle
New Kensington, PA 15068
www.whitakerhouse.com

Library of Congress Control Number: 2023930283

No part of this book may be reproduced or transmitted in any form or by any means, electronic or mechanical—including photocopying, recording, or by any information storage and retrieval system—without permission in writing from the publisher. Please direct your inquiries to permissionseditor@whitakerhouse.com.

1 2 3 4 5 6 7 8 9 10 11 ⊔⊔ 30 29 28 27 26 25 24 23

CONTENTS

SECTION THREE: THE INWARD DISCIPLINES

ACKNOWLEDGMENTS

Writing this book would not have been possible without the friendship of youth leaders around the country. Some of my best friends have been committed to youth leadership for many years. Their contributions in small and large churches across America is a major part of the mission of this book. I am honored to be in youth ministry alongside of some of the best young leaders in the church who are shaping *Next Gen Faith*.

The following youth leaders have shared their time and talents to provide small group discussion outlines at the end of each chapter:

- Taylor Murphy, Grand Rapids First Church, Grand Rapids, MI
- Phil Johnson, Emmanuel Christian Center, Minneapolis, MN
- Joey Silva, Belmont Assembly of God, Chicago, IL
- James Alexander, One Church, Modesto, CA
- Daniel Martinez, Trinity Church, Cedar Hill, TX
- Will Ceaser, First Assembly of God, Dothan, AL
- Lulu Murphy, River Valley Church, Apple Valley, MN
- Quentin Winder, Lakeview Church, Indianapolis, IN
- Jarae Meriwether, Lifepoint Church, Clarksville, TN

- Heidi Rausch, Minneapolis, MN

- Paul Sliwa, Church on the Rock, Wasilla, AK

- Whitney Tellez, Scottsdale, AZ

Thank you all for your insights to help leaders and students get practical in their theology and faith!

INTRODUCTION

We have a crisis in our generation. The crisis is that we are serving a God we do not know.

One of the most alarming research discoveries in the U.S. over the last five years is the plummeting adherence to Christianity and the dramatic loss of a biblical worldview among the last four generations.

It doesn't take much effort to see this decline. Especially looking at Generation Z, the present teenagers and college students, where only 4 percent have a biblical worldview. Gen Z also has the highest number of atheists (13 percent) in any generational set.

In multiple research findings from Barna Group, Pew Research Center, OneHope's Feed initiative, *Christianity Today*, and the American Worldview Inventory, 84 percent of the Silent Generation, born between 1928 and 1945, claimed to be Christian. They gave birth to the Baby Boomers, who then had the children that we call Generation X, who are adult parents today. Research shows that only 67 percent of Generation X claims to be Christian.

We saw the statistics continue to spiral downward when Generation X had their first set of children, the Millennials, who are in their late twenties to early forties today. About 49 percent of the Millennial set identify as Christian. Finally, research shows that the present generation of teenagers and college students we call Generation Z, the youngest set of kids from Generation X and the younger brothers and sisters of the Millennials, now includes 34 percent who would call themselves Christian.

So, in four generations, we've dropped from 84 percent who are Christian to 34 percent who so identify. The faith handoff from one generation to the next has failed miserably.

For example, the youngest children of Gen X, Gen Z teenagers today, sunk into a 4 percent biblical worldview. This capped off a four-generation slide from a 65 percent biblical worldview among the Silent Generation.

The latest research reveals the following revealing statistics:

- 27 percent of U.S. population is Gen Z
- 35 percent of Gen Z consider themselves atheist, agnostic, or no religious affiliation
- 13 percent of Gen Z claim to be atheist as opposed to 7 percent of Millennials
- 50 percent of Christian teens in the U.S. believe Jesus was raised from the dead
- 32 percent of Christian teens in the U.S. believe Jesus is active in the world today
- 46 percent of Christian teens say they never read the Bible
- 45 percent of Christian teens believe all religions have equally valid truths
- 39 percent of Gen Z attend church weekly
- 16 percent of Gen Z say becoming spiritually mature is a goal in their life

PART OF THE PROBLEM IS THAT WE ARE DOING YOUTH MINISTRY IN A NICKELODEON WAY WHILE OUR TEENAGERS ARE LIVING IN A STRANGER THINGS WORLD.

When it comes to the faith of the next generation, youth ministry in America needs a missiology—a plan. We need to change the way youth ministry is done.

Part of the problem is that we are doing youth ministry in a Nickelodeon way while our teenagers are living in a *Stranger Things* world. The church treats young people several years younger than they actually are—with programming like Gaga ball, 9 Square, pizza parties, relational small groups without theological discussions, and sermonettes on The Avengers. Meanwhile, the public school system treats them as young adults, demanding their understanding, discipline, teamwork, and punctuality.

THE CHURCH TREATS YOUNG PEOPLE SEVERAL YEARS YOUNGER THAN THEY ACTUALLY ARE, WHILE THE PUBLIC SCHOOL SYSTEM TREATS THEM AS YOUNG ADULTS.

Young people can handle theology. They can handle the deeper things of God's character and nature. They can understand the Scriptures as easily as they can understand reading, writing, and arithmetic. Do not underestimate the ability and the willingness of teenagers to grasp Christianity and a biblical worldview. The spiritual formation of a generation depends on this.

THE GRAND CANYON

We have a crisis in this generation. We are serving a God we do not know.

It's like seeing photos, watching movies, and hearing people tell stories about the Grand Canyon all of our lives. We get this image in our mind and have an illusory understanding of one of the seven natural wonders of the world. Maybe we even have an emotional connection with the thought of the Grand Canyon. But, in reality, if we have never been there in person, we have never *seen* it.

All of our lives, we have seen the social media posts, the vacation photos, and the advertising pictures of one of the seven natural wonders of the world. We have watched movies, news reports, and *National Geographic* or other magazine or television documentaries of one of the most spectacular places on the planet. But in reality, if we have never stood on the rim of the Grand Canyon, looking at this iconic place as far as the eye can see, we have never seen the Grand Canyon.

Now, relate this analogy to this present generation in America and their relationship with Christianity and God. A generation that has mostly never seen the photos, watched the movies, or heard the stories. A generation that has never had an emotional connection to Christianity. Maybe even a generation that has not been to church or a church youth group.

For the most part, a generation that has never stood face to face with God and *seen* Him.

Among Gen Z, 13 percent are atheist, while 41 percent do not belong to a church. These are the highest statistics in these categories in any generational set.

We have a crisis in this generation. We are serving a God we do not know.

THERE IS A LOT OF RESEARCH DATA AND FINDINGS THAT SHOW HOW LACKING THIS GENERATION'S RELATIONSHIP WITH GOD IS. INCLUDING THE WIDELY PUBLISHED FINDING THAT 13 PERCENT OF GEN Z IS ATHEIST, WHILE 41 PERCENT DO NOT BELONG TO A CHURCH. THESE ARE THE HIGHEST STATISTICS IN EACH CATEGORY IN ANY GENERATIONAL SET.

The crisis is like having a form of godliness, but not having the real thing. We are able to talk about the idea of God, and we may even attend a church. It is like saying with our mouths that we are disciples of Christ but not living like we are His. The form of something is not necessarily the real thing.

The crisis is like knowing who is the president of the United States and being informed enough to say something about his platform and introduce him to a crowd. But in reality, we do not know the president of the United States.

The crisis is like being in the stands at a sporting event. We know the players, can recite the player and team stats, thread fanatically on the socials, and even have the team gear. But we are just spectators; we have never played the game.

The crisis is like having our own favorite genre of music. We have heard the latest release, could quote the entire record, have our Spotify stream top songs of the year, dance to the beat at a club, or scream the lyrics loudly in the car. But we do not know the artists.

I could go on.

In order to understand where I'm going with this book, it helps to be familiar with a few key terms because there are several important concepts that will crop up from chapter to chapter.

THE FAITH HANDOFF

We know the statistics and the research. Today's teenagers, Generation Z, have the highest percentage of atheists than any other generation (14 percent) and the lowest percentage of biblical worldview than any other generation in American history (4 percent).

How did we get here? Over the last eighty years, over four generations, the faith handoff has been abysmal.

Whether the faith handoff continues its plunge into atheism as we raise Generation Alpha will be determined by two things: time and discipleship. Whether America becomes a post-Christian nation or not will be determined by how quickly the family and the church take seriously the theology and spiritual formation that lead to a better understanding of God.

*FROM THE GRANDPARENTS TO THEIR CHILDREN
TO THEIR GRANDCHILDREN, THERE HAS BEEN A
PLUMMETING FAITH HANDOFF IN AMERICA.
BUT WHAT IS MOST CONCERNING NOW IS THE
EFFECT THIS LACK OF A FAITH HANDOFF FROM
ONE GENERATION TO THE NEXT WILL HAVE ON
THE NEXT IN LINE, GENERATION ALPHA.*

God cannot be completely understood through the lens of culture or peer discussions. God and our faith are understood through Scripture and discussions with spiritual elders. It is in the study of Scripture and through discussions with spiritual leaders that we learn language and concepts we cannot learn from culture or limited talks with peers. Christian discipleship and spiritual formation involve a handoff from those who have it to those who do not.

Here are a few important words that every teenager and youth leader must understand regarding Christian discipleship and spiritual formation:

- *Christianity* – the religion based on the teachings and the life of Christ as found in the Bible

- *Religion* – a set of beliefs people have that connects them in relationship to God or a deity

- *Faith* – confidence and trust in a set of beliefs, doctrines, or religious teachings

- *Gospel* – the message of Jesus and Christianity in the Bible books of Matthew, Mark, Luke, and John

- *Rabbi* – a Jewish scholar or teacher of the Bible or other ancient sacred texts (Talmud/Midrash)

- *Acolyte* – one who assists the clergy in religious duties or service

- *Disciple* – the follower or student of Christ who accepts and assists in sharing the faith

- *Biblical worldview* – looking at the world and its issues through the lens of the Bible

There are many things that lead to an understanding of God. Understanding terms and definitions like these is just a beginning.

Once this basic understanding takes place, one can form a biblical worldview—a framework or ethic of understanding the issues and topics in our world through the lens of the Bible and Christianity.

A BIBLICAL WORLDVIEW

What is a *biblical worldview*? Essentially, it's the framework by which we view our life and make sense of the world around us. It's "any ideology, philosophy, theology, movement, or religion that provides an overarching approach to understanding the world and man's relations to the world," says David Noebel, author of *Understanding the Times*.

With such a broad definition, many Americans embrace different aspects of what biblical worldview thinking means to them.

A commitment to the spiritual disciplines outlined in this book would result in a healthy biblical worldview.

A biblical worldview could also be defined as:

- A compilation of absolute moral truth, along with biblical inerrancy and authority
- Understanding the existence of Satan and hell
- The born-again salvation experience of belief in and confession of Christ as the Redeemer who forgives us from our sin and allows us entry into the heavenly kingdom for eternity
- The belief in God as the all-powerful Creator of the heavens and the earth who rules the world today

A compilation of multiple research studies and surveys reveals the following as it relates to statistics on biblical worldview in America:

- One-third of all adults (34 percent) believe that moral truth is absolute and unaffected by circumstances. Slightly less than half of the born-again adults (46 percent) believe in absolute moral truth.

- Half of all adults firmly believe that the Bible is accurate in all the principles it teaches. This includes four-fifths of born-again adults (79 percent) who concur.

- Just one-quarter of adults (27 percent) are convinced that Satan is a real force. Among born-again adults, less than half (40 percent) have that perspective.

- A little more than one-quarter of adults (28 percent) believe that it is impossible for someone to earn their way into heaven through good behavior. Not quite half of all born-again Christians (47 percent) strongly reject the notion of earning salvation through their deeds.

- A minority of American adults (40 percent) are persuaded that Jesus Christ lived a sinless life while He was on earth. Slightly less than two-thirds of the born-again segment (62 percent) strongly believes that He was sinless.

- Seven out of ten adults (70 percent) say that God is the all-powerful, all-knowing Creator of the universe who still rules it today. That includes the 93 percent of born-again adults who hold that conviction.

- In America today, only 9 percent of adults hold a biblical worldview as defined above. Only 19 percent of born-again Christians hold a complete biblical worldview.

- In the end, we are left with the stunning statistic that has placed this current Generation Z at a 4 percent biblical worldview.

This research has supported the lack of a faith handoff in America over the last eighty years. Thus the importance of this book and establishing a biblical worldview for the next generation.

WHAT IS VERY CLEAR BY READING THESE DEFINITIONS OF A BIBLICAL WORLDVIEW IS THAT THE YOUNG PEOPLE OF AMERICA DANGEROUSLY LACK AN UNDERSTANDING OF THE CHARACTER AND NATURE OF GOD.

What does a worldview look like? Picture your worldview as a pair of glasses you might put on that affect how you see the world around you.

Children often view themselves as the center of the world. A secular humanist views the world as merely material and not spiritual. An atheist views the world as godless and rejects all religious beliefs. A Buddhist views life through suffering and penitence or liberation through multiple works and deities. A Muslim views the world through the lens of Quran and the belief that "Muhammad is the Messenger of God." And a Christian views the world through a commitment to Jesus Christ and His Word.

Christianity is a discipleship. It requires a relationship with Jesus Christ. It requires reading the Scriptures and believing they are the inspired Word of God.

THE MAKEUP OF A CHRISTIAN WORLDVIEW

Generally, a worldview would ask some basic questions regarding existence, such as:

1. Where did I come from? (the origin question)
2. Who am I? (the identity question)
3. How should I live? (the morality question)
4. What is my purpose? (the significance question)
5. What happens when I die? (the eternal question)

The importance of asking these questions is undeniable, but so are the answers. And that is where a worldview comes into play. Depending upon your lens or the type of glasses you have on, the worldview you use to answer these questions of life will vary.

So, for example, if we were using a Christian or biblical worldview to answer these important questions of life, it would consist of a certain set of principles or disciplines that we will be talking about in this book. The spiritual disciplines.

Using a Christian or biblical worldview would result in these answers to the five basic questions about existence:

1. I come from God, the sovereign Creator of the universe, who is active in human history (origin)

2. I am a person created in the image of God, who created man male and female in His own image (identity)

3. I should live in the way that is pleasing to God. He has given us the Bible, His Word, for ultimate truth (morality)

4. My purpose is to follow God's Son, Jesus Christ, the Redeemer of mankind, and spread His good news to all (significance)

5. As a believer and follower of Jesus Christ, I will receive eternal life with Him (eternal)

Using this framework or worldview helps a teenager to answer each of the most important questions in life. It shapes our existence by placing value on God as Creator, on our identity as a male or female, on our fallen state and God's redemption, on the Scriptures and not culture as our ethical code, and on eternity and not futility.

Why do I keep hammering home the fact that Gen Z in America has only a 4 percent biblical worldview? Because the vast majority of this generation—96 percent—do not look at the world or its issues through a biblical lens. Their moral standards may be based entirely on what they've learned from culture.

Remember, the Silent Generation—today's grandparents and great-grandparents—had about a 65 percent biblical worldview. There are many reasons for this drop in theological understanding, among them the Bible and prayer being removed from public schools, *Roe v. Wade*, and the sexual revolutions. My hope and prayer is that this book will provide an intentional solution of the failing handoff of the Christian faith from one generation to the next.

The format of the book is a mimic of the classic Christian book *Celebration of Discipline* by Richard Foster.[1] Outside of the Bible, it was the first Christian

---

1. Richard J. Foster, *Celebration of Discipline: The Path to Spiritual Growth* (New York: HarperCollins, 1978).

book that I ever read as a college freshman in 1981. Most leaders in my generation would agree that it's the classic writing on spiritual formation.

Next Gen Faith is a proactive response to the loss of the Christian faith in recent generations. Each chapter focuses on a separate spiritual discipline of the Christian faith. Chapters cover prayer, fasting, worship, study, simplicity, generosity, leadership, the Holy Spirit, and much more. The end of each chapter includes a small group outline for life application of its content, written by one of the great youth leaders around this nation. I've strived to make this book fast-paced and easily readable so that it provides a spiritual and practical help for teenagers and youth leaders.

The book is divided into three sections. The first five chapters are the *foundational disciplines* placed in a life-cycle pattern from daily, weekly, monthly, annual, and lifetime spiritual commitments. The next five chapters are the *outward disciplines* that create a framework for spiritual formation in our public life. The final four chapters cover the *inward disciplines* that help us create a framework for internal spiritual formation.

SETTING PRACTICES TO PROTECT OUR PRINCIPLES

One of the things I learned early in ministry is that we cannot just simply talk about principles. We cannot merely tell the teens and young adults in our youth ministry, "You need to pray more," or "You need to read more," or "You need to evangelize more." It is not enough to tell our students that they need to do more of something they really do not understand. We must show them how. And the way we do that is by giving them *principles* and *practices*.

Most young people know *what* they need to do, but they do not know *how* to do it. And *practices* help them keep their *principles*. You will see both the principle and the practice of these spiritual disciplines in each chapter.

FINALLY

And this is why I have written this book.

We have a crisis in our generation. We are serving a God we do not know.

If we are to reverse the spiraling 4 percent biblical worldview presently in Gen Z and hope to increase the percentage of those with a biblical worldview in the next generation, Alpha, we need a renewed commitment to discipleship and faith formation. A renewed commitment to theology and the works and demonstration of God. A renewed commitment to defining the character and nature of God in youth ministry.

As youth leaders, our work right now must be to create a setting that encourages a relationship between Gen Z and God without borders, ceilings, or fences. To create a place where students can go on a wide open run through the Scriptures without boundaries to discover who God really is.

There's so much more to God than this generation has ever seen. We simply must introduce Him to this generation so they can get a pure picture of God. What they've learned from their peers is not a *pure* picture of God. What they've learned from culture is not a *scriptural* picture of God. And so, presenting teenagers with an accurate biblical perspective of God is the answer to the crisis in this generation.

THE ONLY TEENAGERS WHO DO NOT SERVE GOD ARE
TEENAGERS WHO DO NOT KNOW HIM. BECAUSE ONCE
THEY KNOW HIM, THEY WILL SERVE HIM.

The responsibility of the family, the church, and spiritual leaders is to *define* and *demonstrate* the faith of God to the next generation. As we have seen, over the last eighty years and four generations, we have done a poor job of that faith handoff.

This resource will help all of us create a better biblical worldview in the lives of the young people whom we lead.

SECTION ONE

THE FOUNDATIONAL DISCIPLINES

A cross-less Christianity is a Christ-less Christianity.
—Dietrich Bonhoeffer, *The Cost of Discipleship*

1

DAILY REPENTANCE

(JUSTIFICATION AND SANCTIFICATION)

The central theme of Christianity and the cross is repentance and the forgiveness of sins.

And so, to begin this teenage journey toward spiritual formation, let's begin by looking at the principles and the practices of repentance. We will start with the *principle* of daily repentance and then examine its daily *practice*.

Billy Graham said, "Repentance is not a word of weakness but a word of power and action. It is not a self-effacing emotion, but a word of heroic resolve. It is an act that breaks the chains of captive sinners and sets Heaven to singing."[2]

I could sit and listen to Dietrich and Graham all week long. And on the weekend also.

---

2. Billy Graham, "God's Command to All: Repent!," Billy Graham Evangelistic Association of Canada, November 26, 2020, www.billygraham.ca/stories/gods-command-to-all-repent.

THE PRINCIPLE OF DAILY REPENTANCE

In athletics, muscle memory is everything. Elite athletes will spend most of their time shaping the form and function of a specific skill set. For instance, after playing basketball most of my life, I can walk up to a free-throw line with my eyes closed and still hit seven out of ten free throws. Taking thousands of shots over five decades in the gym, the driveway, or the park set my muscle memory. I understand the placement of my feet, the placement of my elbow above my knee, the release point at the top of my wrist, and exactly how far the rim is from where I'm standing.

In much the same way, we create spiritual "muscle" memory.

When it comes to the spiritual disciplines, we must be willing to set new patterns in our life. These patterns are created the same way I created confidence in my free-throw—through daily practice and repetition. The daily principle of repentance will strengthen your spirit and ultimately create new routines in your life.

> *THE DAILY PRINCIPLE OF REPENTANCE WILL STRENGTHEN YOUR SPIRIT AND ULTIMATELY CREATE NEW ROUTINES IN YOUR LIFE.*

If we could simply see the power in daily disciplines and commitments such as repentance, it would revolutionize our lives. Most young believers understand that the spiritual disciplines are important. However, few ever get to the point of actually practicing them.

If you come from an athletic family or a farming family, or have parents who are teachers or in the military, you know that daily disciplines create success in life. The weight room for an athlete, the field for the farmer, a library for teachers, and basic training for a military home are the settings for real advancement.

Just as there are daily tasks in life that are required for a healthy physical lifestyle—such as getting enough sleep, eating a balanced diet, good hygiene, and exercise—there are many daily commitments that lead to a healthy spiritual lifestyle.

In this chapter, I want to build a case for what I believe to be a foundational spiritual discipline: *daily repentance*. Let's look at what we mean by repentance.

When we look at multiple definitions, we see that repentance means to turn away from sin, a sincere regret of something, the dedication of oneself to an amendment, to be convinced of another way, and to have an after-thought and change of one's mind.

If someone were to tap you on the shoulder, you would turn around and look at them. You wouldn't make a complete circle and keep walking. Our response when the Holy Spirit convicts us of sin should be to simply obey His tap on the shoulder, turn around, and face the other direction.

It is not a 360-degree change in which you spin around in a moment of guilt and continue doing the same thing the next day. On the contrary, repentance is a 180-degree turn in the other direction.

REPENTANCE IS A MOVEMENT AND A DEDICATION TO TURN AWAY FROM SIN AND EVERYTHING THAT'S PREVENTING YOU FROM DRAWING NEAR TO GOD.

Repentance is not simply a moment; repentance is a movement. It is not just a decision; repentance is a dedication. Repentance is the foundation of a healthy biblical life and one of the building blocks of someone's spiritual formation. That's why we place it first as we begin to talk about spiritual disciplines.

THE ABC'S OF SALVATION

Repentance has been called the *Romans Road* or the *ABC's of salvation*. Here are the steps along the way:

- **(A)dmit**. Once we have sinned against God, we must ask God to forgive us of that sin by *admitting* our sin and beginning the process of repentance. Romans 3:23 reminds us, *"All have sinned and fall short of the glory of God."* John the apostle also supports this in 1 John 1:8–9 when he says, *"If we say we have no sin, we deceive ourselves, and the truth is not in us. If we confess our sins, he is faithful and just to forgive us our sins and to cleanse us from all unrighteousness."* The first step in forgiveness is admission.

- **(B)elieve**. After we have admitted our sin and asked God to forgive us, we must *believe* in our heart that Jesus Christ died for our sins and that He is Lord over death, which is the penalty of our sin. Romans 10:9 says, *"If you confess with your mouth that Jesus is Lord and believe in your heart that God raised him from the dead, you will be saved."* That belief is a powerful faith in Christ, who paid for the penalty of our sin.

- **(C)onfess**. It doesn't stop at belief. We must then confess our sin and believe that Jesus Christ is Lord over our life. True repentance is admitting, believing, and confessing that Jesus is Lord of our life.

I love the promise of forgiveness when we have repented. Romans 6:23 says, *"The wages of sin is death, but the free gift of God is eternal life."*

This principle of daily repentance is a foundational ethic for our spiritual lives. Can you imagine the kind of spiritual growth that you would have if you spent a few minutes every day asking God to forgive you of your sins and cleanse you of unrighteousness? That kind of clean-slate living would be liberating!

CALLING SIN WHAT IT IS

Repentance is the pathway to humility before God.

Repentance removes pride from our lives and allows God to then shape us into the person He has created us to be. It is easy to downplay repentance in such a proud culture that exists in America at this time. It is no secret that pride is one of the main obstacles of true repentance. And one of the byproducts of pride is protecting ourselves from shame or guilt by giving new names and terms for our sin. It is very difficult for pride to call sin out, so we come up with slick and comfortable new names for our sin that are easy to live with.

Nobody wants to call sin out anymore because in a moral relativity society, there *is* no sin. And so, instead of drunkenness, we have a *struggle*. Instead of a sexual addiction, we have a *weakness*. Instead of anger or hatred, we have an *issue* we are working through.

> *WE ARE SO RELUCTANT TO CALL SIN WHAT IT IS THAT WE SAY WE HAVE A STRUGGLE, A WEAKNESS, OR AN ISSUE. OUR PRIDE GETS IN THE WAY OF SAYING WE ARE SINNERS.*

This fear or reluctance to call sin what it really is in our society today is driving us away from admitting our depravity and ultimately our need for Christ as Savior. And it has come from a societal shift that will not allow for faith or moral clarity without being cancelled by culture.

Where did all of this come from?

One of the main reasons that we don't believe in sin anymore is because we don't believe in a standard of right and wrong. And when there is no standard, no ethic or framework for right and wrong, then there is no measurement for sin or target for holiness. There can be no principle of repentance unless there is a clear moral code or standard by which we judge our actions to be sinful. By having a clear moral code or standard, we understand when our actions miss the mark, and we have sinned or fallen short. What follows falling short is repentance.

And this is where daily repentance can become a foundational spiritual formation principle.

Daily repentance not only humbles us before God, it places us in right relationship with Him. We must begin our spiritual formation with daily repentance and calling sin, sin, or we will never be able to walk in forgiveness and seek to do what is right and pleasing to God. Of course, God will forgive us, and God loves us. But it is repentance that enables us to ask for that forgiveness and places us in right relationship with our Creator. If we cannot call sin for what it is, we will walk in excuse and never experience forgiveness and the love of God.

MISSING THE MARK

And so, we must begin by defining sin.

The Greek word for sin is *hamartia*, which literally means "to miss the mark." Our actions are like arrows being shot at a target. When they fall short of the target or don't hit the bullseye, we have missed the mark; we have failed and sinned. The target itself is a principle or a standard of right and wrong. Literally, an ethic or a framework.

ONE OF THE ISSUES IN OUR SOCIETY TODAY IS THAT WE DON'T BELIEVE IN SIN—BECAUSE IF WE CHOOSE TO NOT BELIEVE IN A STANDARD OF RIGHT AND WRONG, THEN THERE IS NO SUCH THING AS SIN.

Romans 3:23 says, *"For all have sinned and fall short of the glory of God."* This is a nice word picture of the idea of *hamartia* and missing the intended mark God has for our lives.

Daily repentance should happen when we have disobeyed (or missed) these marks or targets set in the Bible. When we have a relationship with the Holy Spirit, He will bring conviction into our lives when we have sinned or missed the mark of these standards. The immediate response on a daily basis when we have missed the target should be confession and repentance of falling short of this standard.

"RE-ROUTING"

We should be repenting daily when we disobey the moral standard that God has placed before us in the Bible. You could go back to the Ten Commandments, or the wisdom literature in the Psalms, Proverbs, Ecclesiastes, and Song of Songs, or the words of the prophets in the Old Testament, or the Sermon on the Mount from Jesus, the gospels of Matthew, Mark, Luke, and John, and even Paul's epistle writings on living a life in the Spirit and not the flesh from the New Testament. *All* of these are the standard to which God calls His children to believe *and* act upon.

When we have broken these *commands* and stepped outside of this *framework* or missed the mark of these *ethics*, we must repent immediately. Repentance keeps us on track.

I love the concept of midcourse correction. It is simply taking the time to stop ourselves periodically and correct our course. To make sure that we are headed in the right direction and not being distracted along the way.

If you have ever used GPS in your car, you have undoubtedly heard the message prompt, "Re-routing," or some variation. If you happen to make a wrong turn, GPS will correct your route and get you headed back in the right direction. This is a midcourse correction.

Let me give you another example of this concept. If you are driving down the highway and you are one inch off the center of the road, it will not be noticeable at first. But if you continue to drive that way and are gradually inching away from the center of the road, you will definitely notice it when you suddenly find yourself in a ditch! Because course correction is that inch-off adjustment that we make in the wheel of our car to keep us going straight down the highway.

Midcourse correction and repentance will keep you going in the right direction and ultimately can save your life.

CONVICTION AND REPENTANCE

It is not enough to simply be convicted of our sin. We must also complete the conviction with repentance. I have often talked with young people who say they are living in shame and guilt for their actions. I believe this happens because they have been convicted of their sin, but never let repentance run its course.

If we have missed the mark and feel convicted, we must move beyond conviction to repentance. Otherwise, the conviction can turn into shame or guilt and cripple us from receiving God's forgiveness through repentance. It is a powerful revelation in our relationship with Christ to move beyond conviction and into repentance. Because that is where shame and guilt end and where freedom and liberty begin!

> *MOVING BEYOND CONVICTION AND INTO REPENTANCE BRING AN END TO SHAME AND GUILT, REPLACING THEM WITH GOD'S SWEET FREEDOM AND LIBERTY.*

All of us have repeated cycle sins in our life. Cycle sins are those things that we just cannot get over. You know what they are—disobedience to parents, lust, greed, anger, gossip, sexual immorality, or coveting. The only way to be freed from repeated cycle sins is to develop the habit of repeated confession and repentance. Shame and guilt are built up when we do not practice these disciplines. If you meet repeated cycle sins in your life with repeated confession and repentance, you will see liberty and freedom.

THE ROLE OF THE HOLY SPIRIT AND REPENTANCE

The Bible clearly states in John 14–16 that some of the main roles of the Holy Spirit are to teach us the truth, to bring conviction into our lives, to guide us, and to show us the things Jesus taught us. As the Author of the Scriptures, it is the role of the Holy Spirit to bring conviction into our lives when we disobey God's Word.

Here's a great way to illustrate the Holy Spirit's role in our lives: as children, we become fixated on our parents' voices. We remember their words. Over many years of parenting, we are taught what is right and wrong. We are taught how to treat people, and we are taught not to lie or steal. We are taught to watch the words that come from our mouth. Over the years, these things our parents have taught us will always come back to our mind in certain situations.

Have you ever had the voice of your parents echo in your head when you were about to steal something, tell a lie, or commit a sexual sin? I'm sure just about all of us can recall our parents' words of warning in that moment. This is how the Holy Spirit operates. At any given moment, the Holy Spirit brings to our remembrance the things that Jesus has taught in God's Word. That is why it is so important to read the Bible; it gives us a reference for right and wrong!

> *LIKE A GOOD PARENT WARNING US NOT TO SIN, THE HOLY SPIRIT CAN MAKE US REMEMBER WHAT THE BIBLE TEACHES US ABOUT RIGHT AND WRONG.*

We will talk more about the role of the Holy Spirit in our lives in another chapter. However, you will see a reoccurring activity of the Holy Spirit in most of this book because of His role in the spiritual disciplines that we need.

PRACTICES THAT PROTECT THE PRINCIPLE OF REPENTANCE

As you will see in every chapter, we are going to close with practical applications on each topic. So to end this first chapter, here are five practical ways to bring daily repentance into your life:

1. Practice immediate repentance when you know that you have sinned. Do not let a moment go by without asking for forgiveness, even in the middle of your day.

2. It is probably more common for us to repent when we have committed repetitive sins. However, we should make it a habit to also repent of infrequent sins. Left unchecked, these infrequent sins can become more persistent.

3. Learn the difference between sins of omission and sins of commission. Sins of *omission* may be things we did not do that we should have done.

Sins of *commission* may be things that we did that we should not have done. We must ask for forgiveness daily for each.

4. At the end of every day, we should review in our minds any moment that may have brought disobedience into our life and repent of it immediately. Never go to bed with unrepented sin.

5. Journaling or making a list of victories over sin can help us with repentance and forgiveness because it shows us the progress we have made. See the practical group study at the end of this chapter for more on this practice.

FINALLY

Daily repentance is the spiritual muscle memory that we need to build resistance to temptation.

Reading the Scriptures, memorizing the Scriptures, and walking in the Spirit will help us to know what our target is and train ourselves in the ways that we should go. (See Proverbs 22:6.) Additionally, the discipline of repentance will stop Satan and his temptations to sin in our life. When we immediately repent every time he brings the temptation, we will overcome that sin.

The way we break these repeated cycle sins is through repeated confession and repentance.

Over time, do you think Satan wants to bring the same temptation into your life when he knows that you will meet it with immediate repentance? No, he will likely give up and try something else. It's almost like your immediate repentance trains both you and Satan that you know how to defeat temptation.

It's very easy to see how important it is to repent immediately after we have sinned. The Scriptures prove that point. *"God's kindness is meant to lead you to repentance"* (Romans 2:4). And there is nothing like having a clean slate.

SMALL GROUP APPLICATION

Taylor Murphy • Grand Rapids First Church, Grand Rapids, MI

THE PRACTICE OF DAILY REPENTANCE

Remember, Christianity is not a 360-degree change. Actually, that would not be a change at all, but simply turning around for a moment and then continuing in the same direction we were going. That is not repentance.

Christianity and repentance bring a 180-degree turn from the direction that we were going so we head in another direction—the *right* direction. Repentance is exactly what we need to be a disciple and a follower of Christ.

We need daily repentance so that our sins do not build up over time. Too many sins can make us calloused about our ungodly behavior, and we may never get around to complete and total repentance. Daily repentance is a key force against the buildup of layers of committed sin in our life. It also keeps our heart clean before God.

I love how intentionally the Great Awakenings in early America were driven by repentance rallies. Across the eastern United States, Ivy League universities were filled with repentant young people who would confess their sins in public rallies on the university and college campuses. Every week, the surrounding communities would witness these rallies. As a result of these confession rallies, repentance began to turn the tide of sin and wash over our nation with a cleansing wave of revival.

This is one of the settings where the soapbox became very popular. These sturdy wooden crates, which were used to transport bars of soap and other dry goods, became symbols of free speech. Politicians, activists, and preachers would carry around a makeshift soapbox or some other small platform, set it down in the midst of a crowd, stand upon it, and deliver speeches. You would see this in a park, on the street or a sidewalk, or even a populated town square. The soapbox gave the speakers a height advantage over the crowd so they could talk about their political campaign, platform, or issue, or preach the gospel.

In many of these university and college campuses, students stood on a soapbox to publicly repent of their sins. What a powerful discipline of humility, confession, and contrition before God!

Here are some practical ways to apply daily repentance to your life:

1. Write all of your sins down on a whiteboard or a piece of paper. Fill the space up. You may find that easy to do…or exhausting.

2. Look at that chaos on the board or on the paper! It's almost disappointing and freeing at the same time just to look at all of these things going on in your life.

3. What were the conditions or situations going on in your life at the time these sins were committed? Can you recognize a pattern that may have contributed to these sinful acts? For instance, perhaps you didn't do your devotions, listened to the wrong music, spent too much time on social media, or were around the wrong friend group.

4. Now, I want you to begin to repent over each of these things, one at a time. When you are done asking God to forgive you of each sin and you know you have overcome that temptation, wipe the sins off the board or draw a line through them on the paper.

5. Finally, write down several practical things that you can begin to do that will keep you from repeating these sins.

How freeing is that? Your whiteboard has been wiped clean. Your sins have been crossed off. And now you have a list of things that you are going to commit to that will keep you from repeating these sins.

Here are five things that repentance will do in your life. Talk about these with your group:

1. Daily repentance keeps us close to Christ.

2. A lack of repentance hinders our relationship with God by separating us from Him.

3. Repentance strengthens our relationship with God by starting with a clean slate daily.

4.   Repentance brings humility and recognizes God as Lord of our life.

5.   We should repent every night before we fall asleep.

Taylor Murphy is associate pastor of Next Gen Ministries at Grand Rapids First Church in Michigan, having joined the pastoral staff in 2020. Originally from Minnesota, he has a heart to see the next generation follow Jesus passionately and find their God-given purpose at a young age. During his free time, he plays sports, enjoys hanging out with friends, and loves connecting with new people. He studied youth ministry at North Central University in Minneapolis and completed his M.A. in ministerial leadership at Southeastern University in Florida.

If I find in myself a desire which no experience in this world can satisfy, the most probable explanation is that I was made for another world.
—C. S. Lewis, *Mere Christianity*

2

WEEKLY DEVOTIONS

(PRAYER, BIBLE READING, AND FASTING)

One day Jesus was praying in a certain place. When he finished, one of
his disciples said to him, "Lord, teach us to pray, just as John taught his
disciples." He said to them, "When you pray, say: 'Father, hallowed be your
name, your kingdom come. Give us each day our daily bread.
Forgive us our sins, for we also forgive everyone who sins against us.
And lead us not into temptation.'"
—Luke 11:1–4 (NIV)

The only thing the disciples asked Jesus to teach them was how to pray. They
never asked Jesus to teach them how to do anything else. They didn't ask Him
to teach them how to do *miracles*. They didn't ask Him to teach them how to
teach and tell parables to the people. They didn't ask Him to teach them how to
worship. And they didn't ask Him to teach them how to do *evangelism*.

They merely asked Jesus to teach them how to pray. Why? Because I believe it was the *way* Jesus prayed that impacted the disciples the most—not the miracles, or teaching, or the way He worshipped, or His evangelism style.

That is a significant thought about the spiritual life of Jesus. Maybe it was because of His prayer life that Jesus was able to do all of the other things recorded in Scripture. And when we as youth leaders learn the importance of spiritual devotion in prayer, Bible reading, and fasting, it will transform both our own lives and youth ministry, especially if we look at the last twenty years of youth ministry in America.

WHATEVER WE'VE BEEN DOING IN YOUTH MINISTRY OVER THE LAST TWENTY YEARS, WE NEED TO STOP.

It hasn't worked. The biblical worldview of the Millennial and the Gen Z sets has plummeted to 19 percent and 4 percent, respectively. And who knows where Alpha Gen, coming up next, will land on that biblical worldview scale? We have to change because only 33 percent of Christian teens can name half of the Ten Commandments. If we are going to stop the decline and help our youth understand the character and nature of God, we need a commitment to prayer, Bible reading, and fasting that creates a comprehensive theology in youth ministry. Something that is lacking in youth ministry over the last twenty years.

Comprehensive theology is as much a *definition* of God as it is a *demonstration* of God. Comprehensive theology in youth ministry is built through the disciplined devotional life of the youth leader.

I've told the teenagers in my youth ministry many times that if I do not teach them how to *pray*, I have failed them as a youth pastor. If I do not teach them how to *study the Word*, I have failed them as a youth pastor. And if I have not taught them how to *fast*, I have failed them as a youth pastor. We must start evaluating our effectiveness in youth ministry through spiritual formation and not Gaga ball, 9 Square, our social media footprint, our events, or our entertainment quality in the youth service.

SUCCESS IN YOUTH MINISTRY IS DEFINED BY
THE SPIRITUAL FORMATION AND DEVELOPMENT
OF A BIBLICAL FRAMEWORK IN TEENAGERS
FROM CONVERT TO DISCIPLE.

The challenge of youth ministry is to help students develop a life of devotion to prayer, Bible reading, and fasting. These key weekly disciplines are transformative and elementary to spiritual growth. Our students can handle our commitment to a theological emphasis in youth ministry. We have under-challenged teenagers in this area of developing a devotional life, discipleship, and spiritual formation.

We have a crisis in our generation: we are serving a God we do not know.

THE PRINCIPLE OF WEEKLY DEVOTION

There's a difference between devotions and devotion. I know it's a play on words, but it can be easy to go through the *motions* of devotions. It is much better to train your life in the discipline of spiritual devotion to prayer, Bible reading, and fasting than to feel the legalism of having to pray an hour daily, read a chapter in the Bible daily, and fast for one day a week. Devotion is much easier than devotions because it becomes a lifestyle and not a legalistic practice. It sounds like a slight of hand or a magic trick to play with the words, but if you've ever been there, you know what I mean.

I have too often found that when I ask youth leaders about their devotional life, they really cannot define a moment or a place for it. Most people just get around to it or say something like, "Sometimes I pray at night or in the morning or I read before bed some nights. It just happens organically, and I'm not really tied to any routine." It really is random and unplanned. What is important to note here is that we should all have a set time and place for devotion to the spiritual foundations. We will cover that later in this chapter.

OUR FAITH MUST BECOME PERSONAL. WE EACH MUST DEVELOP OUR FAITH AND OWN IT PERSONALLY.

Discipleship and spiritual formation is the responsibility of every teenager. Our faith is not only the faith of our parents or our family; it is not only the faith of our church or our youth pastors. Our faith must become personal. We each must develop our faith and own it personally. Christianity is not just *the* faith; it is *my* faith.

I do not merely want you to know *about* God as a teenager. I want you to *know* Him, to understand His character and nature. But that is going to take time. You will have to work at it.

Sacrifice your time. Isolate yourself at a specific place and time. You will need to persevere when you really do not feel like it. And you must be committed to talk with people who know God and learn from your elders who have been where you want to go spiritually.

Before we look at the practical aspects of having weekly devotion, let's define what we mean by Christian discipleship and spiritual formation in connection with prayer, Bible reading, and fasting.

1. CHRISTIAN DISCIPLESHIP AND SPIRITUAL FORMATION IS THE PROCESS OF ULTIMATELY BECOMING LIKE CHRIST.

The development of a follower of Christ leads to understanding the character and nature of God in prayer, Scripture reading, and fasting. It's a journey that takes time and dedication to understand who Christ is and to commit to becoming like Him. The development of a believer in Christ occurs in both theology and practice. Christian discipleship and spiritual formation is when a follower of Christ becomes devoted to the process in the Scriptures of becoming like Christ in faith and practice. It will turn teenagers into kings and queens to reign with Him. (See 2 Timothy 2:12.) It takes them beyond the elementary principles of Christianity, beyond adolescent spiritual behavior and into adult beliefs and practices.

2. CHRISTIAN DISCIPLESHIP AND SPIRITUAL FORMATION IS THE PROCESS OF UNDERSTANDING AND PRACTICING CHRISTIANITY.

And that process is the responsibility of every teenager. Our faith is not merely the faith of our religion, our parents, our family, our church, or our pastors. Our faith is personal. We must help teenagers understand that Christianity is an ethic, a framework, and a worldview that requires adherence, dedication, and discipline. Ultimately, it requires understanding both the *definition* of and the *demonstration* of our faith. It is when our devotions to prayer, Bible reading, and fasting become devotion. Understanding and action.

3. CHRISTIAN DISCIPLESHIP AND SPIRITUAL FORMATION REQUIRES A DISCIPLINED PLAN OF SYSTEMATIC WORK.

Teenagers have a plan for their homework, their job, and their athletic involvement, so we must also place in them a desire to plan their spiritual formation. If we are going to see teenagers grow up to know God, not just know *about* God, it will take the same kind of commitment to spiritual formation as it does to these other disciplines in their life like school, work, and athletics. To understand God's character and nature will take systematic work.

AN ATHLETE MUST HIT THE WEIGHT ROOM OR THE
PRACTICE FIELD TO BECOME ELITE. A SOLDIER GOES
THROUGH BASIC TRAINING IN ORDER TO PREPARE FOR
MILITARY COMBAT AND ASSIGNMENT.
A FARMER WILL SPEND THE MAJORITY OF THE YEAR
PREPARING AND SOWING BEFORE THE HARVEST.
LIKEWISE, A TEENAGER MUST PLAN FOR THEIR
SPIRITUAL FORMATION.

Teenagers spend so much time in the world and so little time in the Word. If they don't make their spiritual life a priority, the world has a way of conditioning them in its ways. If we are going to see the present spiritual condition of young people in America turned around, it will take youth leaders and youth ministry teaching them how to make their spiritual lives a priority now.

That commitment to unlearn what culture has taught you and learn what Scripture can teach you is one of the great life disciplines. As in other tasks a teenager has, the spiritual life will require a sacrifice of time, isolating yourself at times, and perseverance when you really do not feel like it.

4. CHRISTIAN DISCIPLESHIP AND SPIRITUAL FORMATION IS SUPERNATURAL!

You cannot remove the supernatural from discipleship and spiritual formation in Christianity. And since we cannot deny the characteristic attraction to the supernatural in the Gen Z set, it becomes pretty clear that this is a great mix. Theology and faith is the systematic *definition* of the principles of Christianity, while the supernatural *demonstration* of the principles of Christianity can be passed on from one generation to the next.

MILLENNIALS AND GEN Z ARE DRAWN TO THE SPECTACULAR AND THE SPIRITUAL. THEY'VE GROWN UP WITH THE SUPERNATURAL IN MOVIES, MUSIC, BOOKS, AND TV. IT IS A NORMAL PART OF THEIR LIFE.

Since we cannot separate the supernatural from Christianity then we must make it a part of the everyday life of youth ministry as we work with teenagers. There is no denying that the Scriptures talk about the spiritual life *a lot*. There is Moses meeting with the Spirit, Solomon thinking in the Spirit, Jesus living in the Spirit, Paul walking in the Spirit, Paul and Silas singing in the Spirit, John being in the Spirit, and countless biblical examples of people and their relationship with the Spirit.

With such a great emphasis of the supernatural in Scripture, we must determine to make the supernatural an emphasis in Christians, particularly for our youth. Since we cannot deny the central theme of the supernatural in Christianity and the world of the American teenager, then we must believe God for the same in the Christian and the world teenagers live in.

Most American teenagers and youth culture are completely comfortable with the supernatural. As one of the key definitive traits of the Millennial and Gen Z, they are drawn to the spectacular and the spiritual. We do not have to convince teenagers that the supernatural is for them. They've grown up with the supernatural in their movies, music, books, and television shows. It is a normal part of their life. But what we must show them are the spiritual disciplines that lead to the supernatural doorway to the Spirit.

So, let's look at the principle of these three disciplines: prayer, Bible reading, and fasting.

DEVOTION TO PRAYER

Prayer is mostly misunderstood. One of the things that helped me to understand prayer more fully is this simple little concept: *We do not pray to get, we pray to know.* The purpose of prayer is not only asking God *for something*; it is asking God *for Himself.* The purpose of prayer is not about getting *something*; it is about knowing *Someone.*

For example, we often talk to others about revival and awakening when we should be *praying* for revival and awakening. We must start talking to God about revivals and awakenings. The important work of prayer is the impetus for these moves of God—not talking, teaching, or preaching about revival and awakening. They cannot occur without the hidden work of prayer.

Here are ten lessons I have learned about prayer. Use these practical principles to increase the effectiveness of your prayer life:

1. WE PRAY TO KNOW AND NOT TO GET

This is the greatest lesson I've learned in prayer. Too many of us pray to get something rather than praying to get to know God. God Himself is the reason for prayer. If I get everything else and I do not get Him, I have gained nothing. That is not to say that we are not to ask, seek, and knock until we have received, found, and seen a door opened. But it is critical that we know God before we get anything from God. Sometimes my greatest times of prayer are simply silently sitting with God, asking for nothing but His presence.

When we understand the *relationship* of prayer and not the *benefits* of prayer, we understand a great thing. It is in finding Him that we actually will be moved to a greater prayer life because now we measure the success of our praying through intimacy, communication, and relationship with Him and not whether we received answers to our prayers. The greatest lesson of prayer is that we get God, and everything else is extra.

2. PRAYING ANYWHERE

The more you pray, the more you pray. It really is simple and yet ingenious. Prayer is addictive and only those who have practiced it understand the simple concept that prayer can be done anywhere, at any time. Instead of worrying about having one hour of prayer a day at a set time, we find minutes every hour to devote to prayer.

This does not take the place of dedication and discipline in a certain place. All that's required is the art of relationship or *withness*. Simply being with God anywhere is an important part of prayer. You don't need a building, an altar, or a confessional booth. You don't need a preacher, a worship team, or lights, music, and fog in the perfect setting. Praying has no address, and it has no building where it must take place. Praying is a relationship that can happen anywhere.

3. PRAYING SOMEWHERE

Now look at the opposite of this last principle. As much as we should be praying *anywhere*, we should also be praying *somewhere* and *sometime*. I have found that people who do not have a set time and place do not have a very strong prayer ethic. Sometimes it requires the discipline of time and space. It may be something as simple as setting notifications on your phone to remind you to pray at that moment, or telling others to hold you accountable to your time and space.

The more you pray, the more you pray. Pretty clever, right? I've always felt that when we make prayer a priority, it is much easier to do. When we set a place and time, we make prayer a priority.

For the last twenty-two years, I have prayed at a specific time and place. I decided that I was not going to let prayer be a weakness of mine, so I made a commitment that has guided my devotional life. That has been revolutionary for my desire to pray because I do not have to wait until it happens. I do not interrupt my daily routine to pray. My set prayer time interrupts my daily routine and everything stops.

4. PRAYING WITHOUT WORDS

This should take all of the pressure off prayer. When I hear people say things like, "I don't know what to say," it actually excites me to talk to them about prayer and silence. There are times when my best moments of prayer were just sitting and listening, just getting to know God and not asking Him for anything. The Scriptures warn us not to use flowery speech, vain repetitions, and enticing or persuasive words. (See Matthew 6:7; Luke 20:47; 1 Corinthians 2:4.)

Many times, I have prayed in my mind without audible words and felt His presence as strongly as when I felt like I needed to be *professional* with my words in prayer.

Silence in prayer is like a good relationship. Sometimes you only need to be with somebody and not ever say a word. Our relationship with God is the same way. The greatest benefit of prayer is simply His presence and not my production of words. This is what I mean by silence and simplicity. The Scriptures are filled with the importance of silence.

5. PRAYING WITH OTHERS

I have learned much about prayer by watching others pray. It takes the lid off our own shortcomings and experiences. By watching and listening to others pray, we can learn new ways to explore our own prayer experience. It might be their posture, their tone, their pace, or the content of their prayers. When I pray with others, I have learned so much about *my* relationship with God because of how another person has developed *their* relationship with God.

It also helps to pray with others so that we can be held accountable to our commitment. Praying with another person brings someone else into my life who can call me to the words that I speak. When I pray with another person, it increases my faith for what I am praying because now there are two or three of us believing for our requests.

One of the most important reasons to pray with another person is to have a prayer partner who will challenge you to keep your commitment to prayer. Solomon said in Proverbs 27:17 that a person sharpens a friend just as iron sharpens iron. This is why we pray together.

6. PRAYING AND WRITING

One of my favorite things to do while I'm preaching is to watch teenagers take notes. I love the pressure that it brings to my study and my ministry. If teenagers are going to take the time to write down what I say, I better have taken the time to think about what I'm saying with my words. I will often go up to them after I have preached or taught and ask if I can see their notes. This helps me to see what I'm saying. I have dozens of pictures of teenagers and their notes on my social media pages.

Reading teenagers' notes has also taught me what is important to them. There are times when I've read their notes and thought to myself, *Did I really say that? That's good.*

The other part of taking notes or journaling is writing down prayers. Maybe you write down a prayer from the Scriptures. Or maybe you write down a prayer request or an answered prayer. Writing is another level of learning and retention. By journaling, you can then go back and see what God was doing in your life over the course of time. I have kept nineteen years' worth of journals. I can go back at any time during that span and see what God was doing in my life.

7. PRAYING THE SCRIPTURES

When you do not know what to pray, turn to the Scriptures.

Reading the Bible as prayers can be powerful because we do not have to come up with the language or vocabulary. We simply are praying back to God the

Scriptures that He gave us. It may be the Ten Commandments, the Psalms, or Proverbs, the prophetic prayers of the prophets, Jesus's words in the Sermon on the Mount, or Paul's writings. When we pray the Scriptures, it takes the pressure off trying to come up with something on our own.

Praying the Scriptures also aligns us with truth, faith, and God's promises—a kind of spiritual alignment to the supernatural Word of God. With so much deception and falsehood in modern society, praying the Scriptures centers us in the truth of God's Word.

Praying the truth of the Scriptures equips young people with everything they need to combat the deceit and fraud that is so prevalent in their music, movies, social media, peer influence, education, and the world around them.

8. PRAYING THE CLASSICS

When I was a young youth pastor, I attended a pastors' conference in Indiana. I remember a speaker who talked about prayer and the saints who went before us and paved the way of prayer. As he read the stories of praying saints, I was deeply convicted. Thomas Hyde, Brother Lawrence, Andrew Murray, Kathryn Kuhlman, Leonard Ravenhill, Aimee Semple McPherson, and Corrie ten Boom are all people that I have read about over and over.

IF WE WANT TO GO WHERE WE HAVE NEVER BEEN AND DO WHAT WE HAVE NEVER DONE, WE MUST FIND SOMEONE WHO HAS BEEN THERE AND DONE IT!

There are some things that can only be learned from someone who has been where we want to go and done what we want to do. The language and example of the classic spiritual leaders inspired me to take my prayer to a whole new level at a young age early in ministry. I have every confidence that it will do the same for every teenager reading this chapter!

At that conference in 1985, I committed to a life of prayer. I remember telling God, "I don't want events or attendance to define my youth ministry. I want prayer to define my youth ministry." That conference is the reason why I have had a prayer meeting on a separate night from our youth service at every youth ministry I've served.

9. PRAYING IN THE SPIRIT

Is there a higher form of prayer than praying in the Spirit? I don't think so. These are the purest prayers that we can pray, a conversation with the Holy Spirit on levels that we cannot understand. I love the text where Paul said, *"We do not know what to pray for as we ought, but the Spirit himself intercedes for us"* (Romans 8:26).

PRAYER IS FOREMOST A RELATIONSHIP.
WHEN WE SEE IT THAT WAY, OUR REQUESTS
WILL BE MORE UNDERSTOOD IN THE LIGHT
OF RELATIONSHIP AND NOT WHETHER WE GET
WHAT WE WANT OR NOT.

It's like we are playing chess and not checkers. It feels like we are praying prophetically, and we are one step ahead of what our heart really desires. It actually is a purifying prayer that does not allow for the flesh or selfishness.

Prayer in the Spirit wins the war that we cannot win.

Spiritual warfare is something unseen, yet it is crucial and necessary to success. When the need is severe, prayer must deal with controlling spirits in the situation. When the need is being withheld in contention and war, it may be caused by a supernatural hindrance. Praying in the Spirit wins that war on a level that we may not be able to see in the natural. It will take supernatural praying to contend with the opposition.

10. PRAYER AND WORSHIP

Worship and prayer go together. Turning a teenager's bedroom into a prayer room is all about setting. And nothing may be more important in transforming setting than worship.

You cannot separate worship and prayer. In Luke 19:46, *"My house shall be a house of prayer,"* Jesus used a word translated in Hebrew as *tephillah*—meaning prayer and worship—for what He wanted in His house. The total meaning of the word is "a hymn or supplication and prayer." This is part of the importance of having a prayer and worship life together.

The Hebrew strength of the word *tephillah* is that it places a major importance on the relationship of prayer, hymns, supplication, and worship during our intercession! What a great emphasis for teenagers. A teenager's love of worship is a great combination in their prayer. I believe in the power of worship to change a setting. Worship may be one of the great assists to prayer!

"THERE ISN'T ENOUGH PRAYER"

I love the story of the ministry of Smith Wigglesworth, one of the great evangelists in history.

Smith Wigglesworth was invited to a meeting of ministers in Philadelphia early in his ministry. They asked him to lead a revival and gospel crusade, so he told them he would come and pray with them about the matter.

After about an hour of meeting and short prayers with the ministers, Smith began to pray. And pray. And pray. Several hours later, when he got up from his knees, there was only one organizing minister still there with him. He boldly told the lone minister that he would not be coming to do the meetings in Philadelphia.

When asked why, Smith Wigglesworth simply said, "There isn't enough prayer here to support a revival."

Let that not be said of our youth ministry in America today. Right now, reread these ten practical ways to increase your prayer life. You will see throughout this book that we need practices that will protect our principles.

PRAYER IS NOT OUR PROMOTION

Let me mention something about prayer that has become popular among young leaders today. They say, "When you seek God in private, He will promote you in public."

I really am not a fan of that statement. I understand what people might be saying, but the point of prayer is not promotion; rather, it's the opposite of promotion. Our prayer should be more about intimacy and relationship and deferring humility before an almighty God, not about personal placement or promotion.

This emphasis on promotion can cheapen prayer. It becomes ineffective because it's selfish. It's thinking that God is a cosmic bellhop or a valet service, and all we need to do is ring the bell and ask Him to deliver some dinner to our room or call for the valet to come and bring our car.

I BELIEVE THAT PROMOTIONAL MENTALITY IS PARTLY RESPONSIBLE FOR THE FEELING OF ENTITLEMENT AND ULTIMATELY DISILLUSIONMENT IN YOUNG PEOPLE.

When we don't get what we want in prayer, we blame God. However, in actuality, the foundational purpose of prayer is that we get what we need when we are in relationship with God. Everything else is secondary. Prayer is foremost a relationship with God and then our requests will become clearer in light of that relationship. Remember, we do not pray to get. *We pray to know.* The getting is extra and comes after relationship with God.

Hopefully all of these principles will lead you to a greater prayer life. One of the things I've learned in youth ministry is that we cannot simply ask students to pray more. We must give students this kind of *practical* framework so they can be successful with the *spiritual* disciplines. These practices of prayer will help students to be more comfortable praying. The awkwardness of praying stems from our lack of understanding prayer. By putting some of these things into practice, you will see an increase in your discipline of prayer.

There's another important aspect when it comes to learning how to pray.

INTERCESSION: THE WISDOM FOR PRAYING WITH OTHERS

We have lost the altars today because we no longer *tarry*; we *hurry*. We need to get this place back. I often run to the altar in a service setting. I love the altar. The place of response or decision-making. And it's the place of His presence or meeting.

One of the things that really helped me to understand prayer when I was young was when one of my youth pastors taught me how to pray with other people at the altar. That focus took my mind off always praying for myself and gave me a burden to pray for others. This is called intercession—interceding or praying for someone else.

THE CHURCH ALTAR IS ONE OF THE SETTINGS THAT CAN TEACH US HOW TO PRAY BECAUSE IT'S RESERVED SPECIFICALLY FOR PRAYER AND WORSHIP.

I know that prayer is not contained at the church altar. But it's one of the settings that can teach us how to pray because it's reserved specifically for prayer and worship. I learned to be a person of God's presence at the altar because I spent a lot of time there. That time in His presence taught me how to pray alone and with others.

Our prayer time with another person can be a powerful path to maturity. When you place the needs of others into your praying, you are learning a valuable lesson in prayer. Praying for others can take place in a lot of different settings. One of the most common is when we are in services or gatherings.

Here is some practical advice as you pray with and for others in a service or gathering setting:

- **Listen**. Much of what you want to provide as a prayer support can be gained from being aware and watching what is going on in the service. The themes or topic of the message could be exactly what someone needs in the moment. So if you are listening to what is going on, it will give you a head start and prepare you on how to pray for someone in that moment.

- **Use your discernment**. Allow the Holy Spirit to speak to you first. When your heart is in the right place, you cannot make too many mistakes in prayer. Trust your senses when you are in a spiritual moment and be ready to allow the Holy Spirit to lead you in prayer. Discernment is a gift of the Spirit so ask that God would guide you as you pray.

- **Wait**. When people begin to respond to a message or altar response and prayer time, listening to the speaker or overseer will give you time to pray about the message and a moment or two to think about what you would like to pray for by yourself or for someone else. Additionally, the service leader will often give specific direction for the moment. Waiting for the instructions of the speaker or overseer will help you know how to pray if you are unsure.

- **Watch**. Allow people the freedom to pray on their own initially. Sometimes people may want time to be still or talk with God personally for a few moments. Allow them to respond to the altar time by themselves. We do not always have to immediately pray with someone who has responded to a message.

- **Be available.** If you move toward the front or into an aisle, it will be easier for people to approach you. Moving into an open space like an aisle or altar area may be the invitation for someone that you are willing and ready to pray with them. If you close your eyes all the time, people may not approach you. But if you want to pray for others, keep your eyes open while you are at the altar so you can observe what is going on or see someone who may wish to connect with you. This will make it easier for others to approach you.

- **Ask them**. Asking someone how they would like you to pray for them is a great way to focus on prayer and make sure that you are praying for the right thing. Don't feel like you have to always come up with something to pray. Asking is much easier and begins the relationship with that person.

- **Spirit prayer.** You could simply pray in the Spirit for them and trust God to pray through you for them. Praying in the Spirit is the highest form of prayer that we can pray. The wisdom that follows and the insight received is a supernatural assist to our intercession.

- **Setting**. Your prayer should have the same manner of the setting. For instance, if someone is still, don't shout. If they are broken, don't try to pray joy over them immediately. Sense where the setting is and flow in that pace so that you are not dominant or taking over and bringing attention to yourself. Flow with them until you feel you need to help them change their focus and approach.

- **Laying on of hands**. If you know the person you are praying with, laying hands on them is powerful. It is a transfer and a blessing and a bridge of relationship that can bring comfort and authority to our praying. If you do not know the person well, place your hand on the back of their shoulder and not the top of their head. Do not hold their hands, embrace them, or get too close, which would invade their personal space.

- **Privacy.** When you are praying with someone, it is vital to maintain confidentiality and not betray their trust in you. Keep the requests between you and that other person. Nothing will break your integrity with others quicker than to reveal publicly any information that is personal or private.

- **Hygiene.** Please remember to daily consider your bathing habits, use of deodorant, and breath mints. It may sound trite, but there are plenty of distractions already. Your hygiene shouldn't be one of them.

- **Follow-up**. In future visits to the altar or a casual relationship with someone, ask people how the Lord is working in an area that you may have agreed with them about previously. This can build their faith beyond the moment at the altar.

PROCESS-PRAYING

In our instant society, when meals can be ready after a few minutes in the microwave, all of us need to learn that sometimes, prayer is not a moment. It is a process. This can help in a generation so accustomed to quick answers. The Millennial and the Gen Z set often has a problem with God because His process or timing may not be their process or timing. This generation is so used to instant everything. And when that instant feedback or response is not happening in prayer, it can be devastating to their view of God.

Too often, I have heard young people say something like, "If God doesn't answer me now, He must not care, He must not hear me, or He must not be able to do anything about what I just asked Him for." We have to remove the restraints of time that we have placed on God, or we will never enjoy the process of what takes place in us while God is answering our prayers!

> **WE HAVE TO REMOVE THE RESTRAINTS OF TIME THAT WE HAVE PLACED ON GOD, OR WE WILL NEVER ENJOY THE PROCESS OF WHAT TAKES PLACE IN US WHILE GOD IS ANSWERING OUR PRAYERS!**

God answers every prayer. Sometimes His answer is *yes*. Sometimes His answer is *no*. And sometimes His answer is silence, or God saying, "Wait."

Look at the many examples in Scripture of the time that it takes to get an answer to prayer. The examples of process, patience, and depositing in prayer are many. Remember, much of the asking in Scripture was continual. A look through the Bible will support the importance of learning this concept of process-praying.

IN THE OLD TESTAMENT

- Abraham pleads with God over and over for Sodom (Genesis 18:22–32)

- Hannah praying for years for a child (1 Samuel 1:2–11)

- Elijah prays repeatedly for rain (1 Kings 18:42–43)

- Nehemiah's four months of fasting and prayer before he went to the king (Nehemiah 1:1–2:1)

- Intercessors on the wall who would not give God rest (Isaiah 62)

- Daniel's prayers for his people (Daniel 9)

IN THE NEW TESTAMENT

- Matthew records Jesus pleading with us to be incessant (Matthew 7:7–11)

- Jesus in the garden before His death asking the disciples to pray longer (Matthew 26:38–41)

- Persistence of a neighbor and his desire for help (Luke 11:5–10)

- The widow whose persistence pushes a judge to act on her behalf (Luke 18:1–8)

- Paul asking multiple times for the deliverance of his "thorn" (2 Corinthians 12:7–9)

- Paul's incessant continual prayers for the church (Colossians 1:9)

Here are a few more references to help you understand that prayer is sometimes a process:

> *Then the LORD said, "My Spirit shall not strive and remain with man for-*
> *ever."* (Genesis 6:3 AMP)

Hear me, if God has to strive in His relationship with us, so must we strive in our relationship with Him! I love the emphasis on continually asking, knocking, and seeking that we see throughout Scripture.

> *Ask, and it will be given to you; seek, and you will find; knock, and it will be*
> *opened to you. For everyone who asks receives, and the one who seeks finds,*
> *and to the one who knocks it will be opened.* (Matthew 7:7–8)

Behold, I stand at the door [of the church] and continually knock.

(Revelation 3:20 AMP)

Let's look at the second discipline in this chapter, reading the Bible.

DEVOTION TO READING THE BIBLE

The Bible is the source of the *faith* of Christianity and the Christian. Without it, we lose what is unique about being Christian. If we lose the *faith*, we lose everything.

As youth pastors, we must be constantly thinking of the Bible. If we are spending more time thinking about culture, coffee shops, and clothes, we have lost the foundation of our faith. As teenagers, we must constantly be thinking about the Bible. If we spend more time thinking about our friends, our team sports, or ourselves, we have lost the foundation of our faith. It will take a dedicated commitment and priority to reading the Word of God, the same kind of commitment and priority we put into the other passions in our life, such as friends, sports, self, clothes, coffee shops, and culture.

I WANT STUDENTS TO SEE ME CARRYING A BIBLE RATHER THAN ME ALLUDING TO IT ON THE SCREEN. I WANT THEM TO HEAR ME QUOTE THE WORD IN MY DAILY LIFE.

I want people to look at me and see the narrative of God by the way I live. I want them to see truth, grace, and love in all that I think, say, and do. I want my family and friends to sense God's story in my life every time they see me. I want students to see me walk up in front of them carrying a Bible rather than me alluding to it on the screen. I want my students to hear me quote the Word in my daily life as much as in my messages in the youth setting. I want the Scriptures to be in our music, in my counseling, and in my relationships with teenagers. Otherwise, I have failed them as their spiritual leader.

You will be hearing an important theme often in this book, a recurring thought about the faith handoff from one generation to the next. It's vital that we pass Christianity from one generation to another. That's what the spiritual disciplines really do. The spiritual disciplines are the faith of parents and spiritual leaders being passed on to our children.

THE FAITH HANDOFF IN PSALM 78

Psalm 78 is an iconic chapter in the Bible. King David wrote most of the Psalms. But in Psalm 78, Asaph, one of David's scribes who wrote about a dozen psalms, was recording the history of Israel and God at work in its story.

This psalm is a remarkable read and an important chapter. Asaph was reviewing the responsibilities of the forefathers, the spiritual leaders, and the parents in passing the faith along to the next generations.

Look at all the different ways Asaph defined the words of God and the message of our faith. He uses words like *sayings of old*, *commandments*, *law*, *precepts*, *statutes*, *covenant*, and *testimonies*. This message is not only about *words* though. This message is about *works*. Another set of words that he uses in Psalm 78 is *works*, *ways*, *wonders*, *acts*, and *signs*. It is not just about *principle*; it is about *power*. Our message is both *words* and *works*. We must not only *define* the Word of God to this generation, but we must *demonstrate* the Word of God to this generation.

Why is a spiritual discipline toward the Word of God so important? One of the main reasons is that it is supernatural. It is more than a history book of great sayings from old people. The Word of God is supernatural, and our dedication to it is life-transforming.

THE SUPERNATURAL ASPECT OF THE BIBLE

I recently counted all of the movies and television shows about the supernatural. There are no less than fifty-five that are running right now. It is everywhere in culture. But what is most interesting about this reality is that one of the significant traits of this Millennial and Gen Z generational set is also supernatural. The research has shown that they are totally into the supernatural.

Unfortunately, while the world is familiar with the supernatural, it's mostly foreign to the church. Can you imagine the impact of just one miracle at your high school?

UNFORTUNATELY, THE SUPERNATURAL IS MOSTLY FOREIGN TO THE CHURCH. CAN YOU IMAGINE THE IMPACT OF JUST ONE MIRACLE AT YOUR HIGH SCHOOL?

Because we are both spiritual and natural beings, it makes sense that for us to become like Christ or experience true discipleship, we need the supernatural, transformational power in the Word of God.

The supernatural is really simple. It is the act of God into humankind that began with Genesis and never ceased. The supernatural is God at work in humanity. And I want my students to see the acts of God and not just hear about the history of a God who lived in the past. Sometimes I think it is easier for us to serve an historical Jesus from the first century and forget about the person of the Holy Spirit who is present with us today.

In the last chapter, we will talk about how God is alive and active in history and the world today through the work of the Holy Spirit. Let me just say that the Holy Spirit is the active present theology of God in the Word of God!

Theology really is easy. If you've ever wondered what to preach on in youth ministry, this would be it—the acts and works of God through the Holy Spirit! If all we did was spend an entire series bragging on God and His works and His Word, it would mesmerize a generation. They would be so attracted to His nature and character if we could define Him to them.

Faith is the greatest contribution that one generation gives to the next.

Like Psalm 78, we must hand off the faith of Christianity to the next generations. Faith is our supernatural sustainable gift to them. And because of this, the faith handoff must be the foundation of youth ministry. Why is this so important? Because:

1. We cannot afford to lose the faith of Christianity in the Bible through the generations, so we must see that our faith is the greatest gift we hand to the next generation.

2. The home and the church have lost their emphasis upon the faith of Christianity in the Bible, so we must return to the priority of the Word of God to the family and church.

3. Humanism is the default setting of humanity's thinking, so we must reinsert the faith of Christianity into humanity's thinking, beginning with our children.

4. We live in an age of deception and false prophets, so we must prophesy the truth of Christianity in the Bible to the next generation.

5. Research has shown the dynamic loss of faith from one generation to the next, so we need a dynamic gain of faith from Gen Z to Alpha Gen coming up next after them.

All of this means that the faith of Christianity in the Bible must be the essential message of youth ministry.

YOUTH MINISTRY CANNOT BE SOLELY ABOUT GAGA BALL, 9 SQUARE, AND PIZZA PARTIES ANYMORE. THESE WILL NOT RAISE UP DISCIPLES OF CHRIST.

Youth ministry cannot be solely about games and pizza parties anymore. An event-based youth ministry may get you a decent crowd, but it will not raise up disciples of Christ. Whatever we have been doing over the last ten years in youth ministry, we need to stop. It's not working. It's resulted in a 4 percent biblical worldview in Gen Z. Our latest run of youth ministry in America has produced more atheists and less Christians than any generation in history.

The central problem in young people today is a lack of a biblical worldview, a lack of understanding the nature and character of God. And the only solution to the problem is a comprehensive return of the Bible to youth ministry, the home, and the church. If the present faith—or rather lack thereof—of Gen Z is handed off to Alpha Gen, the younger brothers and sisters of Gen Z, then Alpha Gen is doomed to the same fate as Gen Z today: a dwindling biblical worldview.

That is why we need a spiritual discipline and devotion to the Bible. And ultimately, a definition of the nature and character of God for the next generation. Returning to the Word of God in youth ministry will result in the activity of God and the theology of God born in the generation of young people that we are responsible for today.

We cannot keep on posing excuses to theology in youth ministry. We cannot argue that theology belongs in the sanctuary, that we don't have time to study, that it is the fault of the home, or that teenagers cannot comprehend the deeper things of faith. None of these excuses are good enough for us to just accept the present status quo of faith among teenagers today.

> *WE CANNOT KEEP ON POSING EXCUSES TO THEOLOGY IN YOUTH MINISTRY. EXCUSES LEAD TO UNBELIEF, UNHOLINESS, UNFAITHFULNESS, AND THE UNDOING OF OUR YOUTH.*

Excuses lead to *un's*—*un*belief, *un*holiness, *un*faithfulness, and the *un*doing of our youth, not to mention misbehavior and disobedience. We don't need any more excuses. We need solutions. The deterrent for a lack of theology in youth ministry are the youth leaders across our nation. We are the spiritual leaders of youth ministry in this next generation, and it is our responsibility to create a successful faith handoff in the young people we serve. We are responsible for the many solutions to this plummeting biblical worldview in Gen Z.

MAKING A COMMITMENT TO THE BIBLE

I want to ask youth leaders a few simple questions concerning this commitment to the Word of God in our youth ministries:

PERSONAL QUESTIONS

1. What is your personal discipline when it comes to *reading* the Word of God?

2. And what is your personal discipline as it relates to *studying* the Word of God?

3. Have you seen a *new characteristic or trait of God* in your personal spiritual life?

4. Have you continued to use the *same language* in defining God?

5. How have you made the Bible the *foundation* of the teaching, preaching, worship, and counseling in your youth ministry?

MINISTRY QUESTIONS

1. Do your students sense in you a *love* or *priority* for the Word of God?

2. Are your ministry's messages and series built around a *cultural* or a *biblical* theme?

3. What have you done to add to the *33 percent of teenagers in the church* who can only name half of the 10 Commandments?

4. Does your social media content reflect the Word of God?

5. If your students described their youth ministry in *one word*, what would they say? (If they do not bring up prayer and the Bible, you should be concerned.)

HOW TO INCREASE DEVOTION TO THE WORD

Here are five ways to increase a teenager's spiritual devotion to the Word of God.

1. *The Holy Spirit's role in our life is to bring illumination and revelation as we read the Word of God.* These are often scary words that come with an ethereal or ghostly feel. But illumination and revelation are not meant that way at all here. We simply need a relationship with the Holy Spirit so that He can reveal to us truth as we sit down to read the Scriptures. God's objective and historical past revelation in Scripture cannot be understood accurately apart from the present and personal work of the Holy Spirit. We call that illumination. It is simply the continued work of the Holy Spirit by which He brings enlightened understanding of faith in the Bible and how it should be applied to our life.

2. *Illumination does not eliminate the need for diligent Bible study.* The theologian Bernard Ramm said, "The illumination of the Spirit is no prayer-meeting substitute for the hard work of learning Hebrew and Greek and using the standard lexicons, commentaries and other research materials." Look at it this way: on one hand, Paul encouraged Timothy that *"the Lord will give you understanding in everything"* (2 Timothy 2:7), but on the other, he exhorted Timothy to *"present yourself to God as one approved, a worker who has no need to be ashamed, rightly handling the word of truth"* (verse 15). It takes both illumination and hard work. Paul taught that elders who worked hard at preaching and teaching were *"worthy of double honor"* (1 Timothy 5:17). Far too many preachers enter the pulpit without adequate preparation to rightly divine the Word.

3. *The right tools are an important part of studying the Word of God.* Every student must have a few key tools to help understand what they are reading, such as a study Bible, a commentary set, an expository dictionary of New Testament words, *Manners and Customs of the Bible*, a Hebrew and Greek lexicon, an exhaustive concordance, and Internet capability for research. These are great assists to understanding what you are reading in the Bible.

4. *Set aside study time on a weekly basis.* Set aside one hour a week that is strictly for reading, researching, and thinking about the Bible or a biblical topic using the Bible, books, magazines, newspapers, and the Internet. This can be a revolutionary time of revelation. Once our teenagers read the Word of God, they will do it again! Use a journal or an online app like the YouVersion Bible to gather information while you study. Keeping an

ongoing journal is something you can always go back and read at different times in your life. Keep a life journal that you can record for personal illustrations and spiritual growth stories that will encourage you if you are going through a hard time.

5. *The right setting will create an atmosphere for studying the Word of God.* While I am writing this book, I have instrumental worship music playing. It focuses my mind on the words I want to write and keeps me from being distracted by words I do not want to write! Use music if you enjoy it, stop any appointments for a time, and find a comfortable setting with space, snacks, and no distractions like visitors, outdoor noise, or phones.

Now let's finish this chapter by turning to the power of fasting.

DEVOTION TO FASTING

Over the past few years, there has been an unprecedented number of events that should alert us to a real need for awakening and revival in our world. These events should awaken us to the desperate need for a global spiritual movement that shocks the world.

Look at some of these events: the *disunity* in government, the rise of *racism* in America, *violence* in our schools globally, the recruitment of *child soldiers*, and global *terrorism*, the *financial* crisis, and a global *pandemic*. All of these are taking center stage through news programs, newspapers, media outlets, office conversations, and social media. How does a teen generation overcome the pervasive events that are trying to define their lives?

It will only happen when we raise a new generation of young people who commit to fasting. When we as the spiritual leaders of youth ministry in America call our teenagers to fasting, we will see an unprecedented awakening as never before.

WHEN THE SPIRITUAL LEADERS OF YOUTH MINISTRY CALL OUR TEENAGERS TO FASTING, WE WILL SEE AN UNPRECEDENTED AWAKENING AS NEVER BEFORE.

DEFINING FASTING

One of the things to remember about fasting is that it must be centered on removing food for the purpose of a spiritual replacement. Although there are many things we can remove from our lives for a spiritual purpose—things that delight or attract us—we will not get into the context of media, exercise, or social fasting in this book. Instead, we will focus on the fasting of food specifically for the purpose of a spiritual replacement.

Here are five important principles in the Bible about fasting:

1. Christ did not *command* us to fast, but He did say, *"When you fast,"* implying that we should fast properly. (See Matthew 6:16.)

2. Fasting should reveal what is *controlling* us. That is why fasting in the Bible specifically deals with the appetite. (See 2 Samuel 12:16–17; Psalm 35:13; Jonah 3:5–8; Acts 13:2.)

3. Fasting should be done to make our *spirit* attentive to spiritual things and our *nature* to be inattentive to physical things for a season. (See Daniel 10:2–3; Luke 4:1–13.)

4. When we fast, it creates *spiritual authority* in our lives. Jesus called fasting the key to *"this kind"* of breakthrough. (See Matthew 17:21; Mark 9:29 NKJV.)

5. One of the most powerful results of fasting is *unity*. (See Leviticus 23:27; 2 Chronicles 20:3; Ezra 8:21–23; Zechariah 8:19; Joel 2:12, 15.)

What we do know for sure is that fasting is a special kind of spiritual replacement of a physical or natural appetite or desire. It brings an *urgency*, reveals to us what is *controlling* us, *overcomes* natural desires, and creates spiritual *authority* and powerful *unity*. What we are seeing in our nation today is going to require this kind of tandem spiritual discipline of prayer and fasting for us to see our nation turned around.

BILLY GRAHAM ON FASTING

In his letter, "My Heart Aches for America," Billy Graham, then ninety-three, recalled how his late wife Ruth once expressed concerns about the nation's "terrible downward spiral." She told him, "If God doesn't punish America, He'll have to apologize to Sodom and Gomorrah."

Graham, who preached to more than *two billion* people over the course of his ministry, wrote that we will not see global revival without a new generation committing to fasting. This, he said, was the only one thing that could break the chains over America. He also wondered what Ruth would think of the country today, where "self-centered indulgence, pride, and a lack of shame over sin are now emblems of the American lifestyle."

In this book, and especially this chapter, we are calling youth leaders and young people to a disciplined life of fasting.

WEEKLY FASTING AND PRAYER ON FRIDAYS AT NOON

We are calling all teenagers to fast every Friday at noon. What a movement that would be! As Jesus said in Mark 9:29 (NKJV), *"This kind can come out by nothing but prayer and fasting."* There are some things that we want to see in this generation, but they will not happen without fasting. Without another level of prayer and fasting.

Here is a quick practical guide to fasting in an easy acronym:

FIRST

The journey of a thousand miles begins with one step. Begin with a partial fast of a meal until you are able to see what effect fasting will have on your body. Just start with juices and water for that meal. Do this once a week for a month and then step back and take a look at your physical condition. And ask yourself how the short fast helped you focus on a spiritual target or goal.

ADVANCE

Once you have accomplished the first steps, then proceed with a twenty-four-hour fast or two meals. That means you would fast after dinner on Thursday night and not eat until dinner on Friday night. If you are able, just do water and juice. Don't worry about stomach rumbling or pains; that is simply your body getting used to a new routine. If you are able, it will help if you slow your activity level and lessen the physical exertion during your twenty-four-hour fast.

STAY

Don't make fasting a one-time thing. As you get comfortable with fasting this short time, commit to doing this every Friday, or choose a day that works for you. This is a form of intermittent, cycle, or scheduled fasting. You could even stretch to a thirty-six-hour fast or three meals once you have adjusted your body to fasting. I have chosen every Friday for many years. And because of my discipline of fasting, my fasting has extended into my personal goal of seventy-five days of fasting each year.

TASK

This is the task at hand or the purpose of fasting. To make fasting as effective as possible, make sure that on the fasting day, you focus on prayer, worship, reading, contemplation, silence, and stillness. You want your fasting day routine to be simple, not cluttered with a lot of extras. Remember, you are not just skipping a meal; you are replacing the meal or meals with the discipline of prayer, worship, reading, contemplation, silence, and stillness. I will often choose one task, assignment, or goal to focus on each Friday when I fast.

ING

This is what happens after the fast—the "ing," the measurement or evaluation of what is going on during my fasting. The last *Important Noteworthy Guide* to successful fasting is to make sure you are writing, keeping a journal of your thoughts, readings, and prayers. Make a prayer *request* list and an answered prayer *results* list. This will help you chronicle your spiritual growth and formation. The *ing* is the result.

I want to challenge all of the American Christian teenagers to the greatest prayer and fasting the world has ever seen. How? It's easy. Let me give you some more practical advice about fasting. This might be the kind of things that help you fast better. Break up your prayer and fasting into five days. Something like this:

- **Monday** – fast a meal for yourself and your personal spiritual discipline in the coming week
- **Tuesday** – fast a food item for global leaders, missionaries, church leaders, and Christians
- **Wednesday** – fast a coffee or soda for revival in the youth ministry of America
- **Thursday** – fast eating between meals for family, friends, and your school's faculty and staff
- **Friday** – fast lunch for the lost and unchurched students globally

Over the past two decades, I have called teenagers to fast for lunch on Fridays. Just take a few hours to pray for all the things I've mentioned and review your week during lunchtime every Friday.

You might be thinking that this is hard. You are right. It is supposed to be. If we are going to meet the task of an American renewal, we must ask for the power of the Holy Spirit in our lives. Our natural attempts are not working. And they never have worked, so this should not surprise us. If someone doesn't stand for Christianity now, someone else is going to stand against it. And if the silencing of Christians happens in the U.S, as it already is in other parts of the world, we are going to see persecution in America as we are seeing it in the East.

In my four decades of youth ministry and in reading the stories of previous American Christians, I have seen movements in the U.S. that have approached viral proportions. But what most American Christian teenagers have lacked is true intercession, fasting, and brokenness. Jesus called it a *"this kind"* of ministry. It was different. And that took persistence and sacrifice.

HISTORY IS CLEAR THAT EVERY RENEWAL
OF SIGNIFICANCE IN AMERICA WAS
BEGUN BY YOUNG PEOPLE.

The Spirit is no less powerful and real today. With the rise of so many issues in our world like racism, violence, disunity in government, and terrorism, where are the American Christian teenagers? With all of the saints praying that Western Jesus followers become more aware or engaged on the issue of global persecution of Christians, I want to challenge the American Christian teenager to these simple spiritual disciplines of prayer, Bible reading, and fasting.

Because if we do, the world will see the greatest spiritual awakening we have seen in our lifetime.

SMALL GROUP APPLICATION

Phil Johnson, Student Pastor • Emmanuel Christian Center, Minneapolis, MN

THE CORE

God's Word tells us, *"If we endure, we will also reign with* [Jesus]*"* (2 Timothy 2:12), so congratulations on beginning this journey of becoming kings and queens in heaven!

A decision to change or grow always begins with a decision to *start*! What better place to begin than looking at the core of who you are and the core of growing in biblical literacy. These disciplines that you will learn are important because talent may take you where you want to go, but your *character* and *core* of who you are will be what keeps you there.

As we step into this review, consider these three core disciplines of growing into the king or queen you were created to be.

THE DISCIPLINE OF PRAYER

Prayer is one of those things I always felt like I was doing wrong as a student. I would hear friends talk about how they had heard from God on all these things in their life, and it left me feeling like everyone else had God on speed dial while my number wasn't even saved in His phone. As I got older, I learned that the discipline of prayer is more about developing our relationship with God through intentional and honest conversation, the art of being *present* in His presence.

THE DISCIPLINE OF READING YOUR BIBLE

When I was in high school, I was amazed at how many friends or classmates had opinions about the Bible and what they believed it said. It was the same as someone saying that Popeyes is better than Chick-fil-A but they have never had Chick-fil-A. (My answer is Chick-fil-A, by the way; don't @ me.) Developing a discipline of diving into the Word of God helps us begin to understand *who* God is and *what* He has done for us.

This discipline helps in seasons in which we don't feel like we have heard from God because we can go back to what God has already said. It is a light and a guide in an increasing dark and lost world. Developing this discipline begins with sitting down and opening up your Bible. Start with five minutes and then continue to add time as the habit grows.

Here is another helpful acronym for growing in this discipline that I and many others have used:

- S – Scripture. What book or passage are you reading?
- O – Observation. What stands out to you? Who wrote this? What is happening in this passage?
- A – Application. How can you apply this to your life right now?
- P – Pray. Pray about what you have just read.

As you continue to build on these core disciplines, along with others in this book, not only will you continue to grow in your faith, but you will grow into becoming the king or queen you were destined to be!

OUTLINE

THE DISCIPLINE OF PRAYER

1. Pick a time
2. Create a prayer space
3. Keep a prayer journal
   a. Keep track of requests
   b. Keep track of answered prayers. It is amazing to be able to look back and see all that God has done.
4. Pray about it before you post about it

THE DISCIPLINE OF READING YOUR BIBLE

1. Pick a time and tell a leader right now

2. Make a plan in your small group right now so everyone knows what you are doing

    a. You could start in the New Testament with the gospel of Matthew, Mark, Luke, or John

    b. You could find a plan on YouVersion and follow it

3. Use the SOAP method (Scripture, observation, application, pray)

4. Take notes and journal

5. Find someone you trust to keep you accountable

Phil Johnson is the youth director at Emmanuel Christian Center in Minneapolis, Minnesota. Phil is in his eleventh year of youth ministry and leads a thriving youth ministry at four campuses that comprise Emmanuel Christian Center. He studied at North Central University in Minneapolis. He and his wife Audrey have two sons.

It is clear you don't like my way of doing evangelism. And you raise some good points. Frankly, I sometimes do not like my way of doing evangelism. But I have decided that I like my way of doing evangelism better than your way of not doing evangelism.

—D. L. Moody, evangelist and founder,
Moody Church, Chicago

3

MONTHLY EVANGELISM

(APOLOGETICS)

You will share your faith to the degree that you have been saved.

Now hang on. This is not about degrees of salvation or trying to redefine salvation or put on qualifications for salvation. What I am saying is that if you have experienced a life-transforming salvation, you probably are the first one to share what Christ has done in your life.

In other words, if you were raised in the church and grew up around Christianity but cannot remember the day you were born again, the reality of having a burden for someone else who is lost and unchurched may not be very important to you. Our passion for others to know Christ is directly tied to our own personal transformation we have experienced in Christ.

Now, I can feel the thinking going on with this comment. But what I want you to think about is that if we do not see our faith as valuable, we probably will not spend the time sharing it with someone else.

> **IF WE DO NOT SEE OUR FAITH AS VALUABLE, WE PROBABLY WILL NOT SPEND THE TIME SHARING IT WITH SOMEONE ELSE.**

Simply put, to whom much has been forgiven, there is an obvious burden of responsibility in the kingdom of God to do the same, to pass the faith along. We call this apologetics.

APOLOGETICS

Apologetics is simply the defense and the definition of our faith. It is very important to have a personal apologetic. As a matter of fact, it is much easier to share your faith when you understand its value. That understanding breeds confidence when it comes to evangelism, so having a prepared apologetic ethic or strategy is everything when it comes to sharing our faith.

There are varying views and arguments surrounding the evangelistic ministry of Christianity.

Pluralists say there are many ways to heaven. The *coexist* crowd believes that all of us have the answer. The arguments of the *Buddhist* would be that good karma will help you get to heaven, even though you may not stay there. A *Muslim* would argue that enough good deeds will give you the grace you need when you stand before Allah the Almighty. Additionally, there are others that do not even believe in an afterlife or the existence of a heaven to be gained or a hell to be shunned.

The debate continues and the excuses are varied. We could say that the lack of evangelism is caused by people who attend church without being born again.

Or we could make a case that Christians just don't know how to share their faith effectively. The most dangerous excuse to me is held by Christians who have no burden or desire to share their faith.

Hear me, I am not advocating for Bible thumping and hell-raising dialogue that is insensitive and legalistic. What we need in this generation is to understand the responsibility of our salvation, the practical part of sharing our faith, and seeing the lost with the eyes of Christ.

DIFFERENT APOLOGETIC APPROACHES

We see the American church's approach to evangelism in a few popular mind-sets. I may be generalizing a bit, but I see these mindsets like cars on a highway. The *classic church stream* would find itself in the right lane, moving at posted speed limits and perfectly content to watch everyone else pass them by. The *emergent church stream* would be speeding along the left lane with someplace to go and maybe even missing the point along the way. The *missional church stream* would find itself in the center lane in the middle of traffic, waving at everyone on both sides of them.

ONE OF THE MOST IMPORTANT COMMANDS GIVEN
TO US IN THE SCRIPTURES IS TO SHARE OUR FAITH IN
CHRIST AND TELL OTHERS ABOUT HIS FORGIVENESS.

While some churches and people *overvalue* the discussion, other churches and people *undervalue* the question. Some will contend that we must make people as comfortable as possible. Others say we must bring conviction into people's lives so that they are as uncomfortable as possible. I do agree that *evangelism begins* with relationship and an incarnational presence in culture. We must understand the language, culture, and worldview of a people. But don't forget that *evangelism ends* with the transformation of a person into a disciple. If the question is never called, how can one be saved?

EVANGELISM BEGINS WITH RELATIONSHIP AND AN INCARNATIONAL PRESENCE IN CULTURE. IT ENDS WITH THE TRANSFORMATION OF A PERSON INTO A DISCIPLE.

Don't forget the story of Jesus eating supper with His followers and sinners.

> *A lot of disreputable characters came and joined them. When the Pharisees saw him keeping this kind of company, they had a fit, and lit into Jesus' followers. "What kind of example is this from your Teacher, acting cozy with crooks and misfits?"* (Matthew 9:10–11 MSG; see also Mark 2:15–16)

"Disreputable characters...crooks and misfits." I love that. But what is remarkable about that moment is that Jesus not only sat and ate with them, trying to build relationship with them, but He also preached the gospel to them. What a great model for evangelism from Jesus.

AT SOME POINT, YOU MUST MOVE BEYOND EATING OR PLAYING OR LISTENING OR WHATEVER APPROACH YOU TAKE TO EVANGELISM, AND YOU MUST BRING THE GOOD NEWS.

Let's talk about theology and missiology, or a strategy of mission, a way or method of the discipline of sharing our faith. As the old adage goes, if we fail to plan, we plan to fail.

A THEOLOGY OF EVANGELISM

An important discussion has been going on in our culture for years, specifically within Christianity. It is the conversation about the importance of evangelism and the proselytizing of people to faith in Christ. It stems from the concept in Christianity of the good news of the gospel of Jesus Christ for all mankind. It stems from Christianity's call to eternal life in heaven through faith in Jesus Christ. It stems from the confession of our sins and the forgiveness of those sins through the death and resurrection of Christ. It stems from the mission of the church to reach the lost and make disciples of all nations.

The struggle is real. In our post-modern and progressive society, there is a dangerous discussion and movement to silence our faith. Some claim we should not be going public and should not share our faith with others. But clearly, there is an apologetic mandate in the Scriptures for every Christian.

A true theology of evangelism is really simple. We are all created as children of God. At some point in our life, we have all broken the laws of God, and we need a Savior for the forgiveness of our sins. So, God sent His Son, Jesus, to die on a cross and become the perfect sacrifice for our sins. All we need to do is accept that forgiveness and follow Christ and His commands. One of the most important commands Christ gave us was to share our faith in Him and to tell others about this forgiveness.

ONE OF THE MOST IMPORTANT COMMANDS GIVEN TO US IN THE SCRIPTURES WAS TO SHARE OUR FAITH IN CHRIST AND TO TELL OTHERS ABOUT THIS FORGIVENESS.

Look at this elementary theology of evangelism from the Scriptures:

- **Proverbs 11:30** (NKJV) – *"The fruit of the righteous is a tree of life, and he who wins souls is wise."*

- **Daniel 12:3** – *"And those who are wise shall shine like the brightness of the sky above; and those who turn many to righteousness, like the stars forever and ever."*

- **Matthew 11:28** – *"Come to me, all who labor and are heavy laden, and I will give you rest."*

- **Matthew 28:19** – *"Go therefore and make disciples of all nations, baptizing them in the name of the Father and of the Son and of the Holy Spirit."*

- **Mark 16:15–16** – *"And he said to them, 'Go into all the world and proclaim the gospel to the whole creation. Whoever believes and is baptized will be saved, but whoever does not believe will be condemned.'"*

- **Luke 14:23** – *"And the master said to the servant, 'Go out to the highways and hedges and compel people to come in, that my house may be filled.'"*

- **Luke 24:45–48** – *"Then he opened their minds to understand the Scriptures, and said to them, 'Thus it is written, that the Christ should suffer and on the third day rise from the dead, and that repentance for the forgiveness of sins should be proclaimed in his name to all nations, beginning from Jerusalem. You are witnesses of these things.'"*

- **John 3:5** – "Jesus answered, 'Truly, truly, I say to you, unless one is born of water and the Spirit, he cannot enter the kingdom of God.'"

- **John 15:16** – *"You did not choose me, but I chose you and appointed you that you should go and bear fruit and that your fruit should abide, so that whatever you ask the Father in my name, he may give it to you."*

- **Acts 2:38** – *"And Peter said to them, 'Repent and be baptized every one of you in the name of Jesus Christ for the forgiveness of your sins, and you will receive the gift of the Holy Spirit.'"*

- **Romans 10:9** – *"If you confess with your mouth that Jesus is Lord and believe in your heart that God raised him from the dead, you will be saved."*

- **James 5:20** (NKJV) – *"He who turns a sinner from the error of his way will save a soul from death and cover a multitude of sins."*

Contained in these texts are some of the most important words on evangelism, outreach, and apologetics, the message of the gospel itself, the importance of the messenger, and our responsibility to the gospel. As youth leaders, we need to call our students to a lifestyle of evangelism by preparing them with both the theology (why) and the missiology (how) of evangelism. Understanding these simple texts and the practical steps in this chapter will help young people develop a biblical framework for evangelism and the actual strategy to enact it.

MULTIPLE STRATEGIES

Singular strategies will only reach one type of student. Our evangelism philosophy must go beyond an approach to one circle or set of students. For example, if all I do is use language and events toward the athletes, then I'm only going to reach athletes. We must be willing to create multiple and diverse strategies and approaches to reach all of the kinds or types of students in our community.

A mono-strategy of evangelism is effective to reach one student. But an entire community of teenagers cannot be reached that way. We need a multi-strategy of apologetics to reach the diversity of students in our community.

ONE STRATEGY TO REACH ONE STUDENT IS EFFECTIVE. BUT WE NEED A MULTI-STRATEGY OF APOLOGETICS TO EVANGELIZE THE DIVERSITY OF STUDENTS IN OUR COMMUNITY.

For instance, there are all kinds of teenagers to reach—alternatives, brainiacs, hipsters, artisans, geeks, conservatives, progressives, and different races, genders, and even religious backgrounds. All of these traits require a youth ministry to use varied approaches to reach these students.

Consider these practical steps to building a personal apologetic strategy:

- We should be using a combination of these approaches to reach students: a weekly youth service, discipleship, small groups, evangelism, fine arts, theology, and campus access
- Consider changing up the youth service or create a youth service for a season if you don't have one

- Each approach should include instructing the youth ministry with evangelism tools and training so that every area of the youth ministry understands the responsibility of sharing the faith

- Do not get stuck programming in one of these areas, but spend time using all of these different approaches to reach all of the different tribes of students

The importance of the gospel may be even more vital at this time in world history. We haven't seen an awakening in America for about fifty years. The last spiritual movement our nation has seen came about around 1967 through 1978 in central California. The Jesus Movement, as it was called, was hailed by *Time magazine* as "America's most significant spiritual moment." You can see that reflected on the magazine's cover for June 21, 1971.

But we need to stop having the discussion and debates about awakenings and evangelism and call for the question of the moment!

ROBERT'S RULES OF ORDER

Robert's Rules of Order is a guide to parliamentary procedure and includes a basic rule for every discussion. After a significant amount of discussion, the leader *begs or calls for the question* on the floor or at the table. It's time for the crowd to do something about the issue at hand.

In the same way, I believe it is time to *call for the question* in our culture today.

BUT AT SOME POINT WE MUST ASK PEOPLE
TO ACCEPT CHRIST AS THEIR SAVIOR, TO BRING
THEM TO A POINT OF DECISION.

What is the question? It is to ask that the argument to come to a conclusion, to actually do something about what we have been talking about. I know we value *lifestyle evangelism* in our Western culture, the idea that we should share the gospel and, *if necessary*, use words. Much of evangelism is serving people, loving people, and being an example of the life of Christ every day in our relationships at home, school, work, or the team.

I know the conversations of faith are passionate, and our faith should be seen and heard. But how aggressive should Christians be in sharing their faith? We should have the discussions and then call for the question at hand. When? Listen to the Spirit, and He will give you instruction. And probably pretty quickly. Because today is the day of salvation.

People are more than ready to accept eternal life in heaven through faith in Jesus Christ—*if* we are willing to call for the most important question people will ever have to answer.

The discussion should never cease in a community, but it should come to an end at some point with an individual. When is the discussion going to cease and the question called? If our discussion is truthful and representative of the gospel, the call for the question can come sooner rather than later.

IF OUR DISCUSSION IS TRUTHFUL, LOVING, AND REPRESENTATIVE OF THE GOSPEL, THE QUESTION, "DO YOU ACCEPT JESUS AS YOUR LORD AND SAVIOR?" CAN COME SOONER RATHER THAN LATER.

How much does our faith mean to us?

What is the value of our salvation?

What am I doing to promote my faith?

Apologetics is who we are. Apologetics is a test of my level of relationship with Christ. I realize that *some* people do not share their faith because of ignorance (they don't know how) or pride (they don't want to). But *most* people do not share their faith because of a lack of personal change in their own life.

QUESTIONS TO ASK YOURSELF

- Do I understand my faith?

- Is my faith clear enough to me that I could explain it to someone else?

- To what degree has my faith changed my life?

- If my faith has had such an important impact upon my life, why would I not share it with someone else?

- Could it be that those who do not share their faith with others are the people who have not seen a significant change in their own spiritual lives?

- If I knew that I had twenty-four hours to live, how would it change my approach to sharing my faith?

If you *believe* there is a real heaven and a real hell, it should change the way you *behave*. When you have had a personal spiritual change in your life because of your relationship with Christ, it should compel you to say something to others.

WHY SOME DON'T SHARE THEIR FAITH

In my discussions with students, I have found that many teenagers do not share their faith for various reasons, such as:

- Fear of what people may think about them

- Fear about what to say

- Ignorance on how to answer someone's questions about their faith

- Not knowing any unbelievers

- Not wanting to force their religion on someone

- Lack of a burden for people

As a youth ministry, we must have multiple strategies to counter these reasons and help our students reach their lost friends. We cannot have just one youth ministry strategy when it comes to evangelism. It takes all kinds of people to reach all kinds of people. And it will take all kinds of approaches to reach all kinds of people.

A GPS TO SHARE YOUR FAITH

Here is an easy way to train yourself to share the gospel and your faith using the acronym GPS. Whatever the reason may be that keeps you from evangelism, these are practical principles to help you:

G | KNOW THE GOSPEL

If you understand the gospel in its simplest form, it will be easy for you to share your faith. The basic gospel can be found in the book of Romans. *"All have sinned and fall short of the glory of God"* (Romans 3:23); the wages of that sin is death (Romans 6:23); and the free gift of God is eternal life (Romans 10:9–10). All we need to do is confess our sins and believe in our hearts that Jesus Christ is Lord. This is called the Romans Road. It could also be called the ABC's of evangelism, where *A* stands for "all have sinned," *B* stands for "believe in your heart," and *C* stands for "confess with your mouth."

P | KNOW YOUR PLAN

Most people see evangelism as something uncomfortable that's done either in a public crusade, on the streets, or door to door. But there are so many potential settings for evangelism. It may be using our social media, praying for our lunch, not participating in gossip, or telling someone at work or at school that we will pray for them. Having a plan makes it much easier.

I don't want this to be a lifeless or meaningless routine, but sometimes it helps to have a plan, so try to witness and share your faith with one person each month. Take the first half of the month and pray for one person. Don't even tell them that you're praying for them or try to open any conversational doors. Then, in the last half of the month, you can began to serve that person or tell them that you have been praying for them. You'll be amazed at the conversations that result from a little strategy. Believe me, the Holy Spirit is looking for opportunities to use you!

S | KNOW YOUR STORY

What will best help you connect with a person is your story. Everyone has a powerful story—and people love to listen to stories. The Holy Spirit will use your story to demonstrate the transformation in your life.

Here's a great way to learn your story in one minute: Write your story down on one page or about three hundred words. Do not do more than that. Then reread your story until you have it memorized. That way, it will be much easier for you to know what to say when you're sharing your faith with someone else.

What should you include in your story? Talk about the *old and the new*, the *before and after*, and *darkness and light*. Christianity is all about the old things that have passed away and the new things that have come into your life. Christianity is all about the way you were before you were born again and the way you are now. And if you talk about the dark things in your past such as addictions, doubts, or selfishness, then you must talk about the light things in your life and how you are living today. People understand those concepts very easily.

Let's look at another topic in this chapter on the importance of sharing our faith on the school campus.

CAMPUS MINISTRY AND APOLOGETICS

One of the major concerns of mine in youth ministry is its lack of a presence on public school campuses. For several reasons I will mention in this section, there is a loss of a burden and a strategy to reach teenagers in their context—to see the school campus as a primary mission field. The school campus is *the last tribal stop* of our young people, the place where we can find them gathered in groups for the last time before adulthood. It may be the final place the church can reach these students with the gospel.

A HISTORY LESSON FROM 1962–1963

In 1962–1963, as a result of pressure from the atheist Madalyn Murray O'Hair and others, prayer and Bible reading were officially removed from U.S. public schools. What too many people have erroneously assumed is that this decision was final: no prayer and Bible reading allowed on school campuses. Parenthetically, let me say that's not really a big deal because as long as there are tests in school, there will be prayer in school. Ha! But that is far from the decision that was handed down by the Supreme Court. In fact, in all actuality, this decision has nothing to do with the right of students to exercise their faith on campus.

The removal of organized prayer and Bible reading on public school campuses applies to the exercise of mandated religious activities by school administration and adults, not students. We know that students are praying and reading their Bibles every day there, but we need a greater strategy within youth ministry to reach the campus. To be honest, if there's a will, there's a way.

Here are a few reasons why youth leaders are not on campus:

- *Intimidation.* It certainly can be a scary thing if you do not know anyone or if you have no burden for students. But finding one student, teacher, staff member, or coach can improve your comfort level when walking onto campus or attending an event. Furthermore, it is the *why* that is able to overcome the fear.

- *Lack of a burden.* The *why* is critical, but the *way* is important too. When a youth leader has a burden for the campus, they will solve the time or relational issues, or other obstacles. If a leader can develop a burden for the campus, then there are plenty of practical ways to get them there.

- *No student discipleship.* We haven't produced campus missionaries, which is the easiest way to have an impact on the campus. When we raise disciples, we raise campus missionaries. Theology and apologetics are at the core of our teenagers' lives so they can practice their faith in their context.

- *No model in their own youth ministry growing up.* This is not a new problem. Youth ministry has had a lack of campus access for a long time. Today's youth leaders did not have a consistent model or strategy demonstrated to them when they were teens. It hasn't been in their essence or DNA.

- *Limited by ideas.* Ideas really can be a great instigator here. We have to stop thinking that the only way to access the campus is to speak in a classroom or preach in the cafeteria!

With all of this in mind, let me get practical. Here are a couple dozen ways to have an influence upon the school campus as a youth ministry and have a presence in the setting and culture of teenagers:

- The best way a youth ministry gets on campus is by training and equipping our students as campus missionaries

- Make yourself available to the school for crisis counseling

- Run for school board or other educational positions in government and local elections

- Look to get involved in the myriad of extracurricular activities at school

- Find the Christian para-church organizations that are recognized clubs on campus and have a presence or leadership in them

- Send birthday cards to your students' friends and faculty with your youth ministry name on it

- Use seasonal and holiday themes to attend concerts and plays

- Have students wear youth ministry themed clothing, merchandise, or gear to familiarize the school with your youth group at events or daily at school

- Attending the funerals of youth, school staff, or faculty to build relationships in the school at difficult but important times

- Monitor current events and headlines and be ready to offer lectures, counseling, or intervention

- Pray publicly at community events where school officials are present, such as elections or banquets

- Use your skillsets in many different areas to serve the school, such as coaching athletics, choir, band, theater, officiating sports, speech or debate team, or teaching

- Use school facilities for a Christian concert or seminar

- Have your students promote youth group activities or events

- Encourage your students to invite the youth pastor to classroom as a guest speaker for a religious or non-religious subject

- Organize a Super Bowl party and use the school facilities to host it

- Promote your youth group website on clothing, gear, and stickers for book covers or lockers

- Attend the Fellowship of Christian Athletes, Young Life, Youth Alive, or other campus student-led organizations

- Organize a Seven Project or youth speaker or assembly at your school

- Organize a clean-up crew for after football games to sweep the grounds
- Sing the National Anthem or have the youth choir sing at a game
- Attend or promote the weekly Bible study at your school
- Offer a place at the church for a class to build a homecoming float
- Purchase school T-shirts for a pep rally before an important game and have your youth group wear them
- Provide chaplaincy and prayer before or after a game or school event
- Attend *See You At The Pole* every September or create a monthly *See You At The Pole* meeting

THE LAST TRIBAL STOP

There is one more concept that I want to bring up on the discipline of apologetics and evangelism. It is the importance of the setting of the school campus and what I like to call *the last tribal stop*.

This is the place where we can find teenagers gathered together in sub-groups—by class, age, course of study, athletic teams, interests, and location—for the last time before adulthood. It may be the final place the church can reach these students with the gospel before they leave family and home for a career or college. The school campus may be the last chance to reach teenagers in their peer setting.

I HAVE HEARD YOUTH LEADERS BEGGING STUDENTS TO COME TO THEIR CHURCH, WHILE THE YOUTH MINISTRY IS UNWILLING TO GO TO THE SCHOOL CAMPUS.

Too often, I have heard youth leaders say their local school campus is closed to the gospel, and the youth ministry is not allowed on campus. I've never understood this. I have yet to see a closed campus in my thirty-eight years of youth ministry. Why? Because students have to be on campus. And it is our responsibility as youth leaders to raise campus missionaries who impact the school campus. What I have heard are youth leaders' excuses about getting on the campus. I have heard them begging students to come to their church, while at the same time, the youth ministry is unwilling to go to the school campus.

You have seen in this chapter a myriad of ways a youth ministry can access the school campus. Hopefully these ideas will help you to see the massive value of evangelism there. As youth leaders, we are actually training student missionaries to their home, their workplace, their world, and especially their campus.

FINALLY

Remember what D. L. Moody said at the beginning of this chapter? "My way of doing evangelism better than your way of *not* doing evangelism." It doesn't matter how evangelism and outreach are done. It doesn't matter when or where they are done. All that matters is that evangelism and outreach *are* done.

One of the things that I respect the most about the denomination that I serve is the emphasis upon missions, evangelism, and outreach. We have prayed that the Lord of the harvest would send out laborers, we have served the nations at the felt-need level, built water wells across the globe, provided for humanitarian work globally, given the winds a mighty voice of the gospel, and provided cars, planes, trucks, buses, boats, bikes, donkeys, and sound systems for the gospel to speed the light of Christ to the ends of the earth.

By practicing the principles in this chapter, we can create missional lives, youth who have a plan for evangelism.

I hope this chapter on the spiritual discipline of sharing your faith will help you to see your personal responsibility of *relationship* with unbelievers and bringing people to a *response* to the gospel of Jesus Christ. The discipline of apologetics is at the core of Christianity. And I hope this chapter will help you practically so that you can become more comfortable with sharing your faith.

SMALL GROUP APPLICATION

Joey Silva, Pastor • Belmont Assembly of God, Chicago, IL

> *So for the second time they called the man who had been blind and said to him, "Give glory to God. We know that this man is a sinner." He answered, "Whether he is a sinner I do not know. One thing I do know, that though I was blind, now I see." They said to him, "What did he do to you? How did he open your eyes?" He answered them, "I have told you already, and you would not listen. Why do you want to hear it again? Do you also want to become his disciples?" And they reviled him, saying, "You are his disciple, but we are disciples of Moses. We know that God has spoken to Moses, but as for this man, we do not know where he comes from." The man answered, "Why, this is an amazing thing! You do not know where he comes from, and yet he opened my eyes. We know that God does not listen to sinners, but if anyone is a worshiper of God and does his will, God listens to him. Never since the world began has it been heard that anyone opened the eyes of a man born blind. If this man were not from God, he could do nothing." They answered him, "You were born in utter sin, and would you teach us?" And they cast him out.* (John 9:24–34)

OUTLINE

1. KNOW WHY YOU SHARE

- If you don't care, you won't share.

- Evangelism is an act of gratitude for who God is and what He's done in and through you.

- Romans 9:1–3 says, *"I am speaking the truth in Christ—I am not lying; my conscience bears me witness in the Holy Spirit—that I have great sorrow and unceasing anguish in my heart. For I could wish that I myself were accursed and cut off from Christ for the sake of my brothers, my kinsmen according to the flesh."*

- Do you know the difference between a body builder and a strongman?

  » One works out for show

» The other works out for purpose

2. SHARE WHAT YOU KNOW (NOT WHAT YOU DON'T)

- Some of us don't share our faith because we feel like we don't know enough.

  » Haven't been a Christian long enough

  » Haven't read enough of the Bible

  » Don't have all the answers

- You don't need all of the answers because people do not have all of the questions.

  » Just share what you know

  » And tell someone that you will find an answer for them if you don't know something

- John 9:24–25 (NIV) says, *"A second time they summoned the man who had been blind. 'Give glory to God by telling the truth,' they said. 'We know this man is a sinner.' He replied, 'Whether he is a sinner or not, I don't know. One thing I do know. I was blind but now I see!'"*

- All I know is I was blind and now I see.

  » But how do you explain suffering in the world? All I know is God is with us in it.

  » But how do you explain other religions? All I know is the truth of my religion.

  » But how do you even know that was God? All I know is how I've been changed.

- All you know is *all* you need!

3. SHARE AS YOU GROW

- Don't wait to share about your experience with Jesus.

- » People wrongly assume that they need to grow some more before they share

- » But I believe that we grow as we share our faith

- The healed man has an increasing awareness of who Jesus is.

  - » *"The man called Jesus"* (John 9:11)

  - » *"He is a prophet"* (John 9:17)

  - » A man from God (John 9:33)

- He barely knew Jesus's name.

  - » But the more he shared about his encounter, the more he understood

4. MAKE A LIST

- Write down the names of your friends who are not born again and do not go to church.

- Then, begin to pray for each of them. As Jeff said earlier, choose one person a month to focus on and serve them well.

- In the coming days, look for ways to share your faith with them simply by serving them or even sharing your spiritual story with them.

Joey Silva is the lead pastor at Belmont Assembly of God, Chicago, Illinois, where he previously served as the youth and young adults' pastor. A veteran in youth ministry, Joey has been a strong advocate for evangelism and winning the Chicagoland area for Christ. He has been involved in multiple efforts and organizations to reach people for Christ.

The rabbi is a lost role in the life of modern-day disciples.
If we lose the rabbi, we lose discipleship.
—Dick Brogden, missionary, LiveDead

4

ANNUAL MENTOR

(DISCIPLESHIP AND FOLLOWING)

All of us need someone in our life we are spiritually afraid of.

Now, I understand the gravity of that statement. Stay with me. This is not about the kind of fear that is authoritarian or controlling, worrisome or stressful.

This is the kind of fear that is healthy. It's an awe of someone whom we respect spiritually. You know, a person mature in the faith whom we are willing to let into our life, such as an elder who has permission to say anything to us. Someone who we revere in the faith. Do you have that person?

I have two people like that in my life. They know that I am an open book to them. They are allowed—encouraged actually—to speak into my life at any time. If I am with them, I feel a bit nervous, and it brings me great accountability. In fact, it brings something greater than accountability. It brings an editor into my life to whom I have given permission to say anything to me, ask any question of me, and require the truth from me.

We have a lot of icons in our life, people we do not even know who influence our lives without having access to us—musical artists, movie stars, fashion figures, and other cultural influencers. What about the need for spiritual advisors or rabbis?

This is one of the most critical needs among young people. If we do not have someone who is allowed to practice spiritual discipline and correction in our life, we place a lid over our spiritual formation and growth. Without the aid of a more experienced and disciplined spiritual leader, we are limited to our own awareness.

All of us need someone in our life we are spiritually afraid of.

FOLLOWING THE RABBI

A few years ago, I went to Israel for ten days. One of the highlights of the trip was watching a rabbi and his pupils. It was a remarkable lesson on following. As I watched this rabbi and seven or eight followers, I noticed something very unique and peculiar. The followers kept their eyes on the rabbi almost the entire time they were following him. If he walked, they would walk. If he turned to the right, they would turn to the right. If he turn to the left, they would turn to the left. If he stopped, they would stop. They rarely took their eyes off their leader.

DISCIPLESHIP: COVERING, MENTORSHIP, COACHING

Let's look at the rabbi from a twenty-first century perspective.

What is meant by an annual mentor? It really is the age-old idea of discipleship. And what is discipleship? It is best understood through a couple of terms I like to use.

First, *followship*, or placing yourself under someone else who is more mature than you in the areas that you are interested in. This is the priority of following someone who has a greater commitment and experience than you may have in most areas, such as mental, emotional, relational, and spiritual disciplines. It really is difficult to learn if you are not willing to follow someone else.

The second term is *withness*, or placing yourself alongside of and in the presence of someone else who is more mature than you in most areas that you are interested in. This is the priority of following someone who has a greater commitment and experience than you may have in most areas, such as mental, emotional, relational, and spiritual disciplines.

Both *followership* and *withness* are critical pieces of discipleship. Because discipleship happens in proximity and not distance. Discipleship is really a Christian term. It is basic to Christianity and is the foundation of Christianity. In fact, Jesus termed the word disciple as a follower of His.

> ### DISCIPLESHIP IS BASIC TO CHRISTIANITY; IT'S THE FOUNDATION OF CHRISTIANITY. IN FACT, JESUS TERMED THE WORD DISCIPLE AS A FOLLOWER OF HIS.

Being an heir to God's kingdom doesn't make us a great king or queen one day. We must do the hard work of discipline and gain the experience of leadership before we receive our crowns.

I love the definition of discipleship and following that Jesus gave in Luke's gospel:

> *Whoever wants to be my disciple must deny themselves and take up their cross daily and follow me.* (Luke 9:23 NIV)

> *Whoever does not carry their cross and follow me cannot be my disciple.* (Luke 14:27 NIV)

Breaking down this definition, we see several concepts of discipleship that Jesus defined:

- **Desire** and wanting to follow Christ. At some point in our life, we have to ask ourselves, "What is most important to me?" This is not a small matter. It is a life commitment.

- **Denial** of ourselves. The reality is that we must humble ourselves of pride and take on the life of Christ and His ways. He must increase, and we must decrease.

- **Daily** focus on the message of the cross. This begins with the death of self and the daily choice of life in Christ. This is not a one-time decision, but a lifetime commitment.

- **Discipline** of following Christ closely. This can be done by looking at the Holy Spirit, focusing upon Christ, reading the Scriptures, and watching someone else follow Christ well.

Listening to Jesus talk about this topic is enlightening. It is not about information only. It is about relationship and transformation, following and withness.

INTRODUCING: THE PRESIDENT!

You know, I could introduce you to the president of the United States. I could tell you about his family, tell you his wife's name, the name of his children, some of his life history, and even the principles of his political platform. I could stand at a presidential gala and act like the president of the United States is a close friend with all of the information that I have about him.

But I do not *know* the president of the United Sates.

In the same way, I believe our generation of teenagers is serving *a God they do not know.* They blindly serve a message or a church or a movement...but that is not wholeheartedly serving Jesus. This is a generation that could probably *introduce* you to Jesus, but they are certainly not following Him, serving Him, or becoming like Him in any way.

A LOT OF US SEE FOLLOWING AS THE NUMBER
OF PEOPLE ON OUR SOCIALS WHO WE
FOLLOW OR WHO ARE FOLLOWING US.
BUT REAL FOLLOWING IS CLOSE PROXIMITY, NOT AN
APPROXIMATE NUMBER OF ONLINE ADMIRERS.

Following is the ability to let someone else lead, direct, and guide the way in your life. We all love to lead and be in control, but in order to lead well, we first must follow well.

Can I be blunt? Following will never go out of style. There will always be someone smarter in the room. It may be a teammate, or that best friend who is *perfect*, or it might be a boss, manager, or coworker. But ultimately, there will always be another person who is out in front of us who may have more knowledge and experience than we do. In the same way, there will always be the need for Christ in our lives, the One we are called to follow.

When it comes to social media, most of us never even look at the pages, posts, or stories of *our followers*. However, we spend a lot of time scrolling through our *influencers'* pages, posts, and stories.

If you were to read the whole chapter of Luke 9, you would get an idea of what Jesus meant by following. Does our discipleship reality sound like these statements? Would these descriptions of discipleship that Jesus gave be indicative of the kind of life we are living?

Here are a few of the key phrases that define discipleship in Luke 9:

- Jesus called the disciples to be close to Him
- Jesus gave them power and authority over demons and to heal the sick
- Jesus sent them to proclaim the gospel and to heal
- Jesus told them to take nothing along the way but to be free of everything
- They followed Jesus to a lowly place to talk
- Jesus taught the disciples in all kinds of settings, and they received the gospel from Him
- Jesus created proximity when He prayed with them often
- Jesus emphasized knowledge and relationship by asking them if they knew who He was
- Jesus defined discipleship as following Him and carrying the cross daily
- Jesus told them not to gain the world but to be concerned only with their souls

- Jesus told them not to be ashamed of Him as they followed Him

- God, Moses, and Elijah revealed themselves to the disciples as they spoke with Jesus

- Jesus equated discipleship as childlikeness

- Jesus told them following Him meant being willing to lose everything else

- Jesus told them to proclaim the gospel everywhere

- Jesus told them that once they committed to following Him, they should not look back

Does our discipleship reality sound like these statements? Would these descriptions of discipleship that Jesus gave be indicative of the kind of life we are living?

Luke 9 is an important chapter in the definition of discipleship and following for a teenager. In most youth ministries across the country, there is little attention placed on discipleship and greater attention placed on attraction and entertainment. However, what is very clear in the Scriptures, and especially Luke 9, is the dedication that it takes to lose oneself in the process of becoming a disciple of Christ—to actually die to self and live for Christ. That is not a popular concept in American Christianity today.

TWO CONCEPTS OF DISCIPLESHIP

To complete this chapter, let's look at two concepts of discipleship: first, the *spiritual* understanding of God Himself; and second, the *practical* process of discipleship between one person and another. I like to call these, "Following the Person of Christ, and following a person of Christ." The first concept is ultimate discipleship by focusing upon the nature and the character of Christ Himself. The second concept involves following another disciple of Christ.

FOLLOWING THE PERSON OF CHRIST

Without a spiritual understanding of God Himself, there can be no discipleship. It is the Person of Christ in the picture of spiritual formation. Discipleship cannot be done without Christ as the central figure. When Christ is removed from discipleship, we simply become like someone else or something else. That is not the goal of spiritual formation in Christianity.

Now, God may use a person—we will talk about that in a moment—but we are not becoming like or being a follower of another person. We are becoming like Christ. Without Christ, discipleship is worthless.

THE NATURE AND CHARACTER OF GOD

Let me give you as clear a picture of discipleship as we can. It begins by defining Christ, and then asking ourselves, are we becoming like Christ? This is the crux of Christianity and discipleship. Discipleship is not about meetings and mentors. Discipleship is about following and becoming like Christ. Here is as accurate a description of Christ as we find in the Scriptures:

> [God] *has delivered us from the power of darkness and conveyed us into the kingdom of the Son of His love, in whom we have redemption through His blood, the forgiveness of sins. He is the image of the invisible God, the firstborn over all creation...And He is before all things, and in Him all things consist. And He is the head of the body, the church, who is the beginning, the firstborn from the dead, that in all things He may have the preeminence.*
> (Colossians 1:13–15, 17–18 NKJV)

I fear that as a younger generation and as spiritual leaders, we have a crisis on our hands. We have not passed the faith on to our children. We have raised a generation that is serving a God they do not know. They are blindly serving a historical Jesus, but they do not know the present Holy Spirit.

Colossians 1 is Paul's description of Christ. In about ten verses, the apostle Paul describes Jesus in all of His glory, holiness, perfection, power, and grace. Paul was very clear to define Christ in His supremacy. His defining moment, however, was when Paul described Christ above and beyond and superior to all of creation and even human beings. Paul said Christ was *first*.

I don't believe this generation has seen Christ as *first*. I think they have seen Him differently. Christ has become an add-on. An addendum. A supplement. Something a generation only wants after everything else. But Christ is not a want at the end of our search. No. Christ is our greatest need. He is first. And then everything, everything else, comes after Him. This is what I want this generation to know. That Christ is above, before, and first.

> **THIS GENERATION HAS SEEN CHRIST AS AN ADD-ON, AN ADDENDUM. BUT CHRIST IS NOT A WANT AT THE END OF OUR SEARCH. HE IS OUR GREATEST NEED. HE IS FIRST.**

Our lack of understanding a theology of Christ has led to us believing another gospel. As Gen X and millennials, we have failed to pass the faith of Christ on to Gen Z and Alpha Gen. And the result? We've seen the research and the statistics of the falling biblical worldview in the last three generations. And now we are at the end of one generation, Gen Z, and at the beginning of another generation, Alpha Gen. Unfortunately, the passing of our faith from one generation to the next looks something like this:

- We have passed a powerless Christ to our children.
- We have spoken of a nameless Christ to our world.
- We have neutered a supernatural Christ to our era.
- We have preached another gospel at the expense of the posterity of the gospel of Jesus Christ.

We have raised a generation that does not know Jesus *first*. If we do not pass the Christ of Scripture on to this present generation, it will be too late to reach the next generation. Gen Z desperately needs to take responsibility for Gen A, their younger brothers and sisters. This must become our mandate as spiritual leaders. If we are going to see them grow up to be kings and queens, to become saints, we must show to them the biblical model of Christ *first*.

I don't want to believe another gospel for one more day of my life. I don't want to pass a powerless Christ to my children. I don't want to speak of a nameless Christ to my world. I don't want to neuter a supernatural Christ to my era. I don't want to leave youth ministry in the dark theologically. I don't want one more day of another gospel.

In all of the days I have left, I want to share the Christ of Colossians 1 that Paul defined so clearly to us. Preeminent. Perfect. Powerful. First.

THE GREATEST RESPONSIBILITY OF ONE GENERATION
IS TO PASS THEIR FAITH ON TO THE NEXT.
WE ARE AT THE CLOSE OF ONE GENERATIONAL SET
AND THE BEGINNING OF THE NEXT. WHAT WILL WE
LEAVE FOR THEM TO FOLLOW?

THE GREAT DEFINITION OF GOD BY HIMSELF

Let's look at one more text that defines God in clear language. This is actually the great definition of God about Himself that He gave to Moses:

> And the LORD said to Moses, "This very thing that you have spoken I will do, for you have found favor in my sight, and I know you by name." Moses said, "Please show me your glory." And he said, "I will make all my goodness pass before you and will proclaim before you my name 'The LORD.' And I will be gracious to whom I will be gracious, and will show mercy on whom I will show mercy. But," he said, "you cannot see my face, for man shall not see me and live." And the LORD said, "Behold, there is a place by me where you shall stand on the rock, and while my glory passes by I will put you in a cleft of the rock, and I will cover you with my hand until I have passed by. Then I will take away my hand, and you shall see my back, but my face shall not be seen." (Exodus 33:17–23)

Man, we best learn about God by looking at these Scriptures where God defines Himself to us! I want you to know Him as Moses did, getting as close to His nature and character as you can. But that is going to take time. Work. Sacrifice.

Isolation. Perseverance. Reading the Scriptures. Willingness to talk to people who know God.

A FASCINATION WITH THE SUPERNATURAL

Right now, there are at least fifty-five movies and TV shows with the supernatural theme. One of the top television shows of all time is even called *Supernatural*. It is unavoidable in our culture.

What do Jesus and Imagine Dragons, Coldplay, Maroon 5, Katy Perry, and countless other musicians have in common?

What do Jesus and *A Quiet Place*, *Friday the 13th*, *A Nightmare on Elm Street*, *Isabelle*, *The Walking Dead*, *Stranger Things*, *Us*, *The Avengers*, *Justice League*, and countless other movies and television shows have in common?

It's the supernatural.

There really is a fascination of the supernatural in our society and in the Bible. You cannot take the supernatural out of culture or Christianity. It is innate in our society and in our faith. And it fuels our relationship with God. The supernatural is what draws us to a closer relationship with Christ in discipleship. Now, I do not mean the supernatural *works* of God only. I am talking about the supernatural character and nature of God Himself!

> GOD HIMSELF IS SUPERNATURAL, BEING BOTH DIVINE
> AND HUMAN. THE SUPERNATURAL DRAWS US TO A
> CLOSER RELATIONSHIP WITH CHRIST IN DISCIPLESHIP.

We see this concept of God as supernatural in what is called *the hypostatic union*—that God is both divine and human. He is one God existent in the three persons of the Trinity, who is above the natural that He created. We should not merely be attracted to the works of Christ. Christ Himself is the attraction.

One of my favorite passages of Scripture is found in the Old Testament book of Job. In fact, I wrote about Job in my first book five years ago.[3] In Job 37–42, there is a remarkable review of the supernaturalism of God. He questions Job about His sovereignty more than eighty times and provides an amazing description of Himself. Here is a quick but limited review of other Scriptures, and what they say about our supernatural Creator, His nature, and character:

In the beginning, God created the heavens and the earth. (Genesis 1:1)

Hear, O Israel: The LORD our God, the LORD is one. You shall love the LORD your God with all your heart and with all your soul and with all your might. (Deuteronomy 6:4–5)

The heavens declare the glory of God, and the sky above proclaims his handiwork. Day to day pours out speech, and night to night reveals knowledge. (Psalm 19:1–2)

"You are my witnesses," declares the LORD, "and my servant whom I have chosen, that you may know and believe me and understand that I am he. Before me no god was formed, nor shall there be any after me." (Isaiah 43:10)

For truly, I say to you, until heaven and earth pass away, not an iota, not a dot, will pass from the Law until all is accomplished. (Matthew 5:18)

Truly, truly, I say to you, whoever believes in me will also do the works that I do; and greater works than these will he do, because I am going to the Father. (John 14:12)

There is one God, the Father, from whom are all things and for whom we exist, and one Lord, Jesus Christ, through whom are all things and through whom we exist. (1 Corinthians 8:6)

Finally, be strong in the Lord and in the strength of his might. Put on the whole armor of God, that you may be able to stand against the schemes of

---

3. Jeff Grenell, *#If Job Had Twitter: When Hardship Hits the Palace* (North Charleston, SC: CreateSpace, 2017).

the devil. For we do not wrestle against flesh and blood, but against the rulers, against the authorities, against the cosmic powers over this present darkness, against the spiritual forces of evil in the heavenly places.

(Ephesians 6:10–12)

To reach all the riches of full assurance of understanding and the knowledge of God's mystery, which is Christ, in whom are hidden all the treasures of wisdom and knowledge.   (Colossians 2:2–3)

For there is one God, and there is one mediator between God and men, the man Christ Jesus, who gave himself as a ransom for all, which is the testimony given at the proper time.   (1 Timothy 2:5–6)

Are they not all ministering spirits sent out to serve for the sake of those who are to inherit salvation?   (Hebrews 1:14)

For the word of God is living and active, sharper than any two-edged sword, piercing to the division of soul and of spirit, of joints and of marrow, and discerning the thoughts and intentions of the heart.   (Hebrews 4:12)

You believe that God is one; you do well. Even the demons believe—and shudder!   (James 2:19)

And to the angel of the church in Smyrna write: "The words of the first and the last, who died and came to life."   (Revelation 2:8)

What is interesting to me is that our world has a fascination with the supernatural but the church is foreign to it. Can you see the connection between the supernatural, Gen Z, and Christianity? It is undeniable. It's an almost too easy relationship factor. Gen Z is drawn to the supernatural—and Christianity is defined by the supernatural. What a perfect setup!

The supernatural is a key element in understanding God. Do you see the significance of the supernatural *character and nature of God* and the role it plays in discipleship? The more this generation knows God in His completeness, the more assured I am that they will serve Him. Because if they *seek* Him, they will *see* Him. And if they *see* Him, they will *serve* Him. The knowledge of God fuels our relationship with Him. It is not simply enough to know *about* God; we must *know God*. We cannot serve a God we do not know.

WE SHOULD NOT MERELY BE ATTRACTED
TO THE WORKS OF CHRIST. CHRIST HIMSELF
IS THE ATTRACTION.

One more way to define God Himself and lead others in discipleship is to understand the names of God and how they describe Him, His character, and nature. Discipleship and following is done best in the complete picture of God Himself. We have heard of the popular and more accepted descriptions of the character and nature of God in the Bible:

I AM	Jehovah	Merciful
Grace	Love	Patience/Longsuffering
Goodness	Blessing	Faithfulness

But have you considered the other great definitions of God Himself in the Bible?

Justice	Holiness	Vengeance
Jealousy	Anger/Hatefulness	Fear/Awe
Glory	Heaviness/Weight	Power

I'm sure it would take a detailed run through the verses and the context of each of these descriptions of God before you understand this list. That will have to be another time. But a complete picture of God is always the best picture of God. Remember, God is perfect. So, could He not be perfectly jealous, or perfectly angry, or have perfect vengeance?

I have learned that a complete knowledge of God is the best definition of God and the most effective way to get people to follow Him. Because the knowledge of God Himself is the fuel to our relationship with Him.

We have a problem in this generation; we are serving a God we do not know. But we cannot completely serve a God we do not know. The only people who do not serve God are people who do not know God.

In Christian thought, God is traditionally described as a being that possesses at least four necessary properties. Every teenager should know the following concepts about God:

1. Omniscience (all knowing)

2. Omnipotence (all powerful)

3. Omnibenevolence (all good)

4. Omnipresence (all present)

In other words, God knows everything, has the power to do anything, is perfectly good, and is everywhere.

This is a look at the spiritual understanding of discipleship in the Person of Christ Himself. But what about the practical understanding of discipleship by looking at a person of Christ? Let's move to the last part of discipleship in this chapter.

FOLLOWING ANOTHER PERSON OF CHRIST

As I mentioned at the beginning of this chapter, all of us need someone in our life who we are spiritually afraid of. Someone who can say anything to us and has access to our life. A person who we respect and view with awe, a willing editor in our life.

Ultimately, discipleship requires a process of one person of spiritual maturity and experience in relationship with another. Remember the importance of proximity, following, and *withness* that we talked about earlier. These are important relational attributes of discipleship. The rabbi's relationship to his disciples is really ideal.

This can be illustrated in the difference between accountability and editing. We need more than an accountability partner in our life; we need an editor. Let me explain.

The saying, "Leave it on the floor" has become a popular phrase for athletes who give their all and hold nothing back. But originally, it was used to describe a scene that was cut from a movie in the film editing process and left on the floor.

When you have a mentor who's an editor in your life, you can be sure that they remove situations that would detract from God's plans for you!

Dietrich Bonhoeffer once said that much of Christianity has been corrupted with a "false faith" that is capable of nothing. It is powerless because it lacks Christ. It is the responsibility of spiritual leaders to deposit a real faith into the next generation. When discipleship is taken seriously and intentionally, we will cease to pass a *false faith* on to the next generation and assure them that they have a real faith.

JESUS STRESSED OUR NEED FOR RELATIONSHIP. EVEN THOUGH CHRIST IS EVERYTHING AND WE ARE COMPLETE IN HIM, WE STILL NEED ONE ANOTHER.

That is the responsibility we have to *"one another"* in the Scriptures and Christianity. It's really a powerful truth that Jesus stressed our need for relationship. I understand when people say things like "I only need Jesus," but that simply is not true. We need each other too. It is a mystery of Christianity that even though Christ is everything and we are complete in Him, we still need one another. Christ said, *"A new commandment I give to you, that you love one another: just as I have loved you, you also are to love one another"* (John 13:34).

Look at the language of the Scriptures and the value they place on community and belonging. We must not forget that the discipline of following is found throughout the Scriptures and is a foundational core value in the kingdom of God. We cannot separate relationship from discipleship or discipleship from relationship.

THE PROCESS OF DISCIPLESHIP AND MENTORING

If we don't have a plan in place for our mentoring relationships, it will be hard to measure their success. Every teenager should get one person every year to speak into their life—an annual mentor. This person could be a parent, pastor, spiritual leader, family member, coach, teacher, or neighbor. But every year, get someone who is more spiritual than you to mentor and train you in the ways of God and Christianity.

It helps to find mentors who are experienced in the things you want to experience. Because if you want to go where you've never been and do what you've never done, you have to first find someone who has been there and done it!

A PRACTICAL GUIDE TO MENTORING

I use an eight- or ten-page pamphlet I created to work with those I mentor. It's served as a practical guide to a healthy mentoring relationship and is a great way to start your formal mentoring relationship with someone. Every mentor should have a structure like this to follow. You may use this content to create your own resources for mentoring and discipleship.

Trust me, it does neither of you any good to just hang out and chat. You need a structured document that guides the process of mentoring so that you can effectively measure your success and progress. The most productive scenario would be to include the following content in the mentoring process and discussions.

PERSONAL BACKGROUND

- Age, education, hobbies, and interests
- Family bio
- Work or vocational information
- Discuss the formative events in the person's life

This will ensure the mentee feels comfortable with your relationship as the mentor as you begin meeting together. In time, there is a foundation of trust to lay the discussions upon.

PERSONAL MISSION STATEMENT

- Have the mentee write out a personal mission statement in one sentence (thirty words or less)

- What would be the goal of their life?

- Look at complexity versus simplicity. Find out what kind of things are getting in the way of the success of that life goal and be willing to eliminate anything outside the lines of the mission statement.

Make sure that the mentee understands their life purpose. Many of the problems in our lives exist because of busyness and unfulfilled purpose.

PERSONAL GIFTS OR CHARACTERISTICS

- List two strengths, abilities, or talents that we need to magnify

- Where do you find the most joy?

- We must accentuate the strengths and gifts that people have because that is where they are unique and will see the most fruitfulness

Exposing the strengths of a person will cause them to be radically awakened to the possibility they are not gifted with just shortcomings, but also have God-given strengths.

PERSONAL MEETING DESIGN

- Each meeting should have a single topic of discussion. Focus on one issue in each meeting so that both of you have optimal growth.

- Meetings should be thirty minutes long and leave the mentee wanting more rather than feeling the meeting is too long and wearisome.

- Balance the amount of *lecture* or *lesson* that you bring as a mentor. Much of what we want to accomplish will be done in a discussion-oriented format.

- Plan the frequency of the meetings (weekly, biweekly, monthly, or seasonal)

Set up an agenda for the meetings based on the discussions from the *personal* questions and the *initial spiritual* questions that follow. You will find that much of what someone is dealing with can be handled by the end of these initial meetings. In order for this meeting design to work well, you should create a schedule and then email or text it to the mentee so that there is sufficient time to prepare for the meetings.

Initial Spiritual Questions

- On a scale of one to ten (one being low and ten being high), where was your spiritual life and devotion six months ago? Comment using two or three sentences.

- On a scale of one to ten (one being low and ten being high), where is your spiritual life and devotion as we speak? Comment using two or three sentences.

- What are the things in your life that you are concerned about? (These may be things like relationships, lack of spiritual disciplines, or indicators that failure is on the horizon.)

- There are sins of *commission* (things you have done) and sins of *omission* (things you have not done). Define two of each in your life right now.

- What are the most formative moments in your life? These could be positive or negative moments.

FINALLY

The more we know God in His completeness, the more assured I am that this generation will serve Him. Because if they *seek* Him they will *see* Him, and if they *see* Him they will *serve* Him.

At the beginning of this chapter, I quoted Dick Brogden: "The rabbi is a lost role in the life of modern-day disciples. If we lose the rabbi, we lose discipleship." Unfortunately, those rabbis are too many of the youth leaders across our country who have lost the importance of personal discipleship of a generation. I am not blaming youth leaders only for this lack. The home bears much of the blame as well...but that is for another book.

We lost personal discipleship in youth ministry the last twenty years. We went to small groups and the model of youth ministry in the early part of this century, but forgot to bring discipleship and mentoring into the small group.

Understand, I am not blaming small groups for this lack. I am blaming *poorly run* small group ministry for this lack.

Our youth ministry in the 1980s consisted of dozens of small groups—but we had a move of God in those living rooms that students will never forget. After hearing a lesson from the Word of God in small group host homes, I remember students all over our city lying on their faces before God, worshipping with an acoustic guitar, prophesying and praying over each other, and inviting their friends into these small groups. And then they would eat, drink, and play games if they had any time left before they had to leave. The emphasis was on spiritual formation talking about Jesus and not chat time.

IN TOO MANY PLACES, SMALL GROUPS TODAY
HAVE BECOME HANGOUTS WITH CHAT SESSIONS
ABOUT LIFE WHERE A LEADER SPENDS MOST OF THE
TIME TALKING AND STUDENTS NEVER ENTER INTO
DEEP SPIRITUAL CONVERSATION.

I've been in small groups across the nation and have witnessed the change first-hand. Many youth ministry small groups include conversation, food, games, and very little theology or accountability to the spiritual life. Youth ministries all over the country stopped doing a youth service, rally-type large crowd event and moved to small group-based programming—kind of like what our teenagers are doing seven hours a day at school.

And what did this get us? A shocking spiraling drop of the biblical worldview in the Gen Z set that hit rock bottom at 4 percent, down from 19 percent in the Millennial generation before them. Sure, the blame for this lies squarely on unhealthy homes too. But youth ministry cannot escape this responsibility of the plummeting biblical worldview in Gen Z. And for what happens in Alpha Gen to follow.

All of us need someone in our life who fills us with spiritual shock and awe. Discipleship and following is one of the most critical needs among young people in the twenty-first century. If we do not get teenagers to allow someone into their life who is allowed to practice spiritual discipline and correction in their life, we place a lid over Gen Z and their spiritual formation and growth. That leaves us with a bleaker outcome for Alpha Gen coming up right behind Gen Z.

If we fail to take seriously the command of Christ to *"go therefore and make disciples of all nations"* (Matthew 28:19), we fail the important mission of the church to pass the faith on to our children, and their children, and their children. We must lead our students to *the person of Christ* in discipleship and lead them to *a person in Christ* who can help them bring the spiritual discipline and correction they need to become disciples and not just fans.

SMALL GROUP APPLICATION

James Alexander, Campus Pastor • One Church, Modesto, CA

Following is the discipline of mentorship, coaching, and accountability. Usually we view following as a box we check off when we are young, with the hope that we will one day graduate from the necessity of a leader in our lives. But I challenge you to embrace mentorship, seek it out, and pursue people to coach your life, to both hold you accountable and cheer you on as you reach milestones.

Those who embrace the blessing of following will quickly find themselves met with a mechanism called accountability. We often think accountability is only needed for someone who has an addiction—to drugs, alcohol, pornography, gambling, or anything else. Such people need an accountability partner to help them not give in to the addiction. However, we all need a mentor, someone who can provide us with spiritual guidance.

There are three simple things you can do to change how you view accountability and how you can apply this to your own life:

1. See accountability as the bread that holds the sandwich and all its contents of who you are together.

    » Imagine trying to eat your favorite sandwich without the bread! It would be messy and chaotic; you would lose half the contents. There would not be enough napkins in the world to clean it up. As a sandwich needs bread, our lives need accountability.

    » Like the sandwich illustration above, what is another analogy for accountability?

2. Find an adult who is older, smarter, and more experienced in the thing you are interested in.

    » Make sure they are in the career you want to have one day

    » This person or group of people are key to your success as they will apply a healthy pressure that keeps you aligned to what is right and is true as a follower of Jesus

    » What two people come to mind?

3.   Move beyond accountability and into editing relationships.

   » What does an editor in your life look like?

   » What are two things you need someone to help you change?

4.   Find a peer who can be accountable to you

   » You need to have someone to mentor who is under you

   » Give freely from the things you have learned

   » Who are the peers or friends who you can become a leader and mentor to?

James Alexander is a campus pastor at One Church in Modesto, California. He has a passion for discipleship and spiritual formation for the next generation. James received his bachelor's degree in pastoral ministry at William Jessup University. He and his wife Chelsey have two sons.

Corrupt the young. Get them away from religion.
Encourage their interest in sex. Make them superficial
by focusing their attention on sports, sensual entertain-
ments, and trivialities. By specious argument cause the
breakdown of the old moral virtues: honesty, sobriety, and
self-restraint.
—Vladimir Lenin, *How to Destroy the West* (1921)

5

LIFETIME OF
SEXUAL PURITY

(SEX AND SEXUALITY)

If we are going to win a generation, we must help them solve the worst of their problems.

It's pretty clear that Lenin's prophetic writing has been realized step by step as we have watched a generation walk in corruption, leave the church, explore sexual immorality, and focus upon other things than Christ.

Perhaps no other spiritual discipline will require you to be so focused than this one on sexuality and identity.

The sexual lives of teenagers are under attack every day from multiple sources that vie for the attention of young people in dramatic fashion. If Gen Z can control this area of their life, they have conquered an army set against them.

The devil knows he cannot steal God from us. So, he stole the next important thing from us—love. And when the devil stole love from us, he stole sex. When love is removed from sexuality, we get a dangerous and new counterfeit for sexuality, one that is defined by a loveless sexual revolution.

Before we get into the importance of the discipline of sex and sexuality, let me give you a quick definition of a sexuality revolution so we can all be on the same page as we begin. We will deal with a complete spiritual and theological perspective of sexuality later in this chapter, but let's look at more natural teleological definitions of the terms first.

SEXUALITY DEFINED

Here are several definitions of sexuality as we begin this journey:

- "The quality or state of being sexual: the condition of having sex; sexual activity; expression of sexual receptivity or interest especially when excessive" —*Merriam-Webster*

- "The quality of being sexual, especially sexual orientation and behavior" —*The Free Dictionary*

- "The feelings and activities connected with a person's sexual desires" —*Oxford Dictionary*

- "Sexuality is just one of those things you are born with, you do not choose it, it's just part of who you are." —*Urban Dictionary*

The importance of the definition of sexuality suggests there is a complementary and natural use of sexuality. You could combine the definitions and come up with "the sexual expression and behavioral feelings that you are born with." Quite an interesting edit from those dictionaries. Basically, sexuality is comprehensive and entails a spectrum of topics because sexuality is wide-reaching.

Which brings us to the definition of a revolution.

REVOLUTION DEFINED

You may have heard of the Cultural Revolution, the American Revolution, the French Revolution, or certain other global revolutions. But the sexual revolution we are going through now, aided by the social media revolution we are experiencing in America, may be the most sweeping revolution of our time.

The teleology of a revolution is interesting. In a compilation of its definitions, it means a radical, turnaround, dramatic, wide-reaching overthrow, grand change, or replacement of something with another. When a revolution is under way, it brings not only change to the government and structure of a nation, it also brings change to its society and ultimately its people.

A REVOLUTION COULD BE A RADICAL CHANGE IN SOCIETY'S CODES, LANGUAGE, AND MORALITY. OFTEN, THESE CHANGES TAKE PLACE FROM EVENTS OR A MOVEMENT THAT GAINS POWER.

What we've seen in the last twenty-five years in America is a swift change because of the influence of the information technology age. From the political, sociological, entertainment, corporate, educational, familial, and religious settings, we have seen sweeping changes reshape the landscape of our nation—and ultimately the world.

And so, when you place sexuality and revolution together, you can see how this can impact a generation.

WHAT IS A SEXUAL REVOLUTION?

One of the cultural realities of the Millennial and Gen Z sets is that they are living in a real and historic sexual revolution—maybe the most impacting, society-shifting tsunami to ever hit the shores of youth. This revolution is undeniable in its effect. It is true America has gone through several sexual revolutions, but the one that the Millennial and Gen Z sets are growing up in now is undoubtedly epic in its impact.

As has happened in the wake of other sexual revolutions, the response of a generation to this one remains to be seen. Right now, the sexual revolution is winning the war on youth in the twenty-first century.

A sexual revolution changes thought, language, and behavior. Look at it this way: a sexual revolution changes *thought* through overwhelming, comprehensive counterculture, and then changes *language* by challenging classic definitions with emerging language definitions. A sexual revolution then changes *behavior* by changing thought and language. It really is chilling to see radical shifts in thought, language, and behavior as we see today.

A SEXUAL REVOLUTION CHANGES BEHAVIOR BY CHANGING THOUGHT AND LANGUAGE. IT REALLY IS CHILLING TO SEE RADICAL SHIFTS IN THOUGHT, LANGUAGE, AND BEHAVIOR AS WE SEE TODAY.

This is why we are placing such a great emphasis upon sexual discipline for youth.

What has been a double curse is that during the present sexual revolution in America, it just so happens that there is also the compounded effect of the loss of theology and a biblical worldview at the same time! So, we must prepare this generation with the spiritual tools to build a biblical worldview of sex. If we can help teenagers focus upon a healthy sexuality ethic, we help them win their greatest war in the twenty-first century.

Every generation has had its sexual revolution, and there have been changes in every culture because of sexuality. It's been a rapid onslaught—from the way people think, the way they dress, the historical burning of bras, the student movement in the 1960s, traditional churches' rejection of "Jesus Freaks" in the Seventies, birth-control pills, rap music, the loss of censorship in movies, the rising acceptance of nudity in the 1990s, and the proliferation of sex on mobile devices.

Today in America, maybe the most astounding and dramatic movement or shift has taken place in the Millennial and Gen Z sets. It is alarming to see the downward spiral of the theological framework in young people. All of the studies are proving this, none clearer than the 2018 Barna Group findings showing Gen Z with a 4 percent biblical worldview. This loss of theology has had a lot to do with the rise of the sexual revolution in America.

THE YOUNG PERSON WHO CAN CONTROL THEIR VESSEL AND THE TEMPLE THAT GOD HAS GIVEN THEM WILL BE A POSITIVE INFLUENCE ON THEIR GENERATION.

This is why it is so important to have a disciplined biblical understanding of sex and sexuality. The young person who can understand a scriptural ethic, know how to communicate it, and control their vessel and the temple that God has given them will truly be a positive influence on those of their generation who are unable to control themselves.

It seems with every revolution has come a free run away from the Bible and a worsening of the values. We have watched the government take a step back by redefining marriage, watched the media take a step back with little censorship, witnessed our schools create progressive sex education in the classroom, taking parents out of the equation when it comes to abortion, and watched gender identity definitions broaden.

Through all of this, our own twenty-first century sexual revolution has put all of the other revolutions in America to shame. And it's pretty clear why this has happened.

REASONS FOR A SEXUAL REVOLUTION

There are several reasons for the rise of the present sexual revolution in America, including:

- The influence over time by progressive education

- A loss of conservative censorship in the media

- An entertainment industry pushing the envelope toward progressive morals

- Humanistic and postmodern thought breakaway from conservatism

- The dramatic loss of theology in the Millennials and now Gen Z

- The silence of the home and the church on the sexual revolution

Each of these influences have contributed to the social and sexuality changes we are seeing in our nation right now. But undeniably, one of the main reasons why we see such an overwhelming and comprehensive counterculture of sexuality rising in America is because of the communication age that we are living in.

It is so much faster and easier to bring about change because information does not have to travel through relational networks on the ground, a telephone call, or written communication between friends. Today, information travels immediately through conference calls, convention meetings, radio and television broadcasts, and innumerable social platforms and apps that are instantly accessible globally in the palm of our hand.

THIS INFORMATION AGE HAS CREATED A BREAKAWAY FROM THE CLASSIC AND CONSERVATIVE AVENUE, STEERING YOUTH ONTO THE MODERN AND PROGRESSIVE MAINSTREAM FREEWAY.

I'm sure if you could have shown a photo of this present sexual revolution to your grandparents fifty years ago, they would have thought a three-ring circus came to town.

In a world that is polytheistic and polysexual, believing in a spectrum of gods and sexuality, we could use some standardization or truth in the world. We must jump off this modern and progressive mainstream freeway and back onto the classic and conservative avenue, or the next roadway we take will be even more dangerous.

PRACTICAL THEOLOGICAL SEXUALITY

We need teenagers to develop practices that protect their principles. If we are going to raise disciples, we must help young people conquer the sexual *desires* in their life with sexual *disciplines* in their life.

Here are ten key practical ways to bring sexual discipline into your life as a teenager:

- Create a theology of sex. You can get this from my previous book *GenSeXYZ* by reading the chapter on "A Theology of Sexuality."[4]

- Create sexuality standards. When I talk about *standardization*, I mean common sense biblical absolutes. The Western mind has no room for that kind of closed spiritual code or belief, but it *is* freeing.

- Limit your social media to an hour a day and make sure that you have someone who is able to check your search and communication practices.

- Understand that the first look is free but the second look will kill you. What do you do if your eye or ear is summoned by temptation? The next move is yours—and it is the most important one.

- Do not go into your boyfriend or girlfriend's room. Imagine a sign on the door that reads, "Danger!" Decide right now that you will not enter that private place.

- If you are at a boyfriend or girlfriend's home, make sure that the parents are home, or another adult is present, keep the lights on in any room you are in, do not lie down under a blanket, and avoid the kind of movies or media that could arouse either of you.

- Tell your parents, guardian, or an adult where you are going on a date so that you can be found or get a ride home if needed.

- Purify your Spotify. Music is one of your greatest assists in keeping your mind, body, soul, and spirit pure.

---

4. Jeff Grenell, *Gen SeXYZ: Love, Sexuality & Youth* (New Kensington, PA: Whitaker House, 2021).

- Group date to take the pressure off from single couple dating, which creates isolation and leads to greater temptation.

- Memorize key verses in the Bible that help you with the spiritual discipline of your sex life. I share seven of them later in this chapter.

THE DATING RELATIONSHIPS OF TEENAGERS

If we are going to win this war, we have to fight the battles, and that requires a systematic discipline in the most critical part of a teenager's relationships—the discipline of dating.

The answer to dating behavior begins with theology and not just physiology.

As it relates to dating, the central principle I have shared with teenagers for decades is they do not *need* each other. As much as students think they need another person, we have to help teens understand their most important relationship on earth is their relationship with God. When that relationship with God is right, every other relationship they have will be right. One of the lessons I learned a long time ago was that two halves don't make a whole in relationships. Two people must bring their whole selves into the relationship to make it whole.

> TWO HALVES DON'T MAKE A WHOLE IN
> RELATIONSHIPS. TWO PEOPLE MUST BRING
> THEIR WHOLE SELVES INTO THE RELATIONSHIP
> TO MAKE IT WHOLE.

Over the years, people have bashed dating and given the same concept another name, such as courting, group relationships, or even the process of engagement. I'm not here to rally against dating. There are principles that, if applied to the practice of dating, can make dating an important part of adolescent development.

Here are a few principles teenagers need to have when it comes to a disciplined dating life. I've given them the acronym *D.A.T.I.N.G.*

- **Date** God first. Then every other relationship will be right. Help teens understand the most important relationship to them is Christ. If that relationship is right, then a dating relationship will be right also.

- **Ask** the parents. Teach teenagers to meet the parents or guardian, and then to ask for permission to date someone. Talking to the parents or guardian first will bring some accountability to the relationship. Getting to know the parents is like getting to know the child. To be honest, this step may stop a lot of bad things from happening.

- **Talk.** When you are on a date, never stop talking. Keep talking. Just talk. May there never be silence. Talk. See what I mean? Bad things happen when you stop talking. Plus, talking will help you to get to know each other and know whether you would like to do this again. Are you interested in someone's intellect? Are you interested in their beliefs? Are you interested in the goals they have for their life?

- **Information must be shared**. Things like time or curfew, what you are doing, where you are going, and who you are with. Another piece of information you should have is your *list* of what you want in a relationship. If someone doesn't match this information, don't date. This basic information will help your dating immensely.

- **Never be alone**. Never go into each other's bedroom alone, never turn the lights off, never lie under a blanket, never put the car in park if you both remain in it, never go beyond kissing, and never drop her off without walking her to the door.

- **Group dating is critical to development**. It can show teenagers how different people treat each other, how to handle relationships with different types and kinds of people, and take the pressure off performing or finding something to do.

THE PURITY AND VIRGINITY OF TEENAGERS

I'm sure you have seen the T-shirts and merchandise that are pro-virgin. A popular clothing line says boldly, "Virginity Rocks."

A few years ago, a middle school student in Wentzville, Missouri, got into trouble for wearing a sweatshirt with the "Virginity Rocks" logo. The principal told the student to remove the sweatshirt or turn it inside out. He was also told he would be suspended if he wore it to school again.

What is interesting about this story is that dozens of students have been threatened with the same action from schools around the country for simply wearing the popular shirts. Are we so afraid of offending people that our attempts at political correctness are threatened by a slogan that supports virginity? What does this say about the condition of our society?

ARE OUR ATTEMPTS AT POLITICAL CORRECTNESS THREATENED BY A SLOGAN THAT SUPPORTS VIRGINITY? WHAT DOES THIS SAY ABOUT THE CONDITION OF OUR SOCIETY?

The Wentzville School District in suburban St. Louis told the CBS television station that covered the incident, "The district's policy regarding student dress provides opportunities for our administrators to address student attire that is potentially disruptive to the educational environment."

Sometimes I cannot even wrap my mind around the lack of common sense in our society.

Let me finish this chapter with several sexual disciplines for teenagers.

THE DISCIPLINE OF SCRIPTURE MEMORIZATION

Gen Z has shown a more conservative approach to having sex before marriage, but they have replaced that trend with other behaviors that are sexually explicit. So how can we help teenagers today live a more conservative sexual lifestyle?

How can a young person keep their way pure? By keeping it according to the Word of God. (See Psalm 119:9.)

Obviously, we have given practical principles of discipline in this chapter, but let me give you a few more biblical principles and Scriptures I have used to help encourage and strengthen teenagers when they are struggling with their purity.

- Look at the strength of the Word to overcome temptation and the pain of falling into sexual sin: *"Do not depart from the words of my mouth. Remove your way far from her* [the immoral woman], *and do not go near the door of her house, lest you give your honor to others, and your years to the cruel one"* (Proverbs 5:7–9 NKJV).

- Here is God's prescription for living holy and pure as a young person: *"How can a young man* [or woman] *keep his* [her] *way pure? By guarding it according to your word. With my whole heart I seek you; let me not wander from your commandments! I have stored up your word in my heart, that I might not sin against you"* (Psalm 119:9–11).

- The key word Paul uses here is *aselgeia* or "unbridled lust and excess": *"The night is nearly over; the day is almost here. So let us put aside the deeds of darkness and put on the armor of light. Let us behave decently, as in the daytime, not in carousing and drunkenness, not in sexual immorality and debauchery, not in dissension and jealousy. Rather, clothe yourselves with the Lord Jesus Christ, and do not think about how to gratify the desires of the flesh"* (Romans 13:12–14 NIV).

- When we are tempted, Paul says: *"Flee from sexual immorality. Every other sin a person commits is outside the body, but the sexually immoral person sins against his own body. Or do you not know that your body is a temple of the Holy Spirit within you, whom you have from God? You are not your own"* (1 Corinthians 6:18–19).

- Paul emphasizes repentance when we have sinned: *"I fear that when I come again my God may humble me before you, and I may have to mourn over many of those who sinned earlier and have not repented of the impurity, sexual immorality, and sensuality that they have practiced"* (2 Corinthians 12:21).

- Here is a great reminder of the place for sexual relations: *"Let marriage be held in honor among all, and let the marriage bed be undefiled, for God will judge the sexually immoral and adulterous"* (Hebrews 13:4).

- Peter reminds us to avoid compromise or fitting in with the crowd: *"You have spent enough time in the past doing what pagans choose to do—living in debauchery, lust, drunkenness, orgies, carousing and detestable idolatry. They are surprised that you do not join them in their reckless, wild living, and they heap abuse on you"* (1 Peter 4:3–4 NIV).

These are some great principles to build a teenage life upon. Commit these to memory, and you will be able to stand against the temptation in our culture. Remember, the sexual revolution is not going away. It has steamrolled its way into town undeterred. It will take a supernatural response and discipline to stand against the sexual revolution and its temptations.

This next discipline is about as practical as you can get—and probably a good practice for all of us.

THE DISCIPLINE OF REDEEMING SOCIAL MEDIA

To redeem your social media is another effective way to create sexual discipline.

All of the sociological research models place teenagers on their mobile device around five to six hours a day and in front of all screens (television, computer, and iPads) about nine to ten hours daily. These *screenagers* today spend more time on their phones but have less apps than their older brothers and sisters, the Millennials. We cannot stop this media wave crashing on our kids.

WE CANNOT STAND IN THE WAY OF THE RUSHING CULTURAL TRAIN PUSHING FORWARD WITH INCREASING CREATIVITY AND FORCE BY SIMPLY HOLD UP OUR FIST IN PROTEST.

The proverbial ant in front of the train is fruitless in its effort to stop this loco-motive. In other words, we cannot stand in the way of the rushing cultural train pushing forward with increasing creativity and force by simply hold up our fist in protest.

Rather than trying to stop this social media force, it is much wiser to put our efforts into redeeming everything for the purposes of God through a disci-plined lifestyle toward media. That means teaching teens how to use their media for good, and us understanding that these tools may be the easiest way to communicate the gospel to a digital generation. It's speaking their own language.

The Mills and Gen Z are growing up in the aftermath of a lot of problems that have swept through their culture. Present cultural issues such as the broken family, an age of terror and war, a divided government, a media and entertain-ment industry that has lost censorship, school and campus violence, the opioid crisis, rising university costs, racial tensions, the overwhelming imbalance of social media platforms, and the COVID-19 pandemic have all left their mark on this generation.

With a disciplined sexual ethic on their social media, this generation has a powerful opportunity to leave their mark of purity on America.

Here's a last discipline that when practiced becomes a powerful pattern of purity in a teenager's life. It is the discipline of creating new patterns and habits that will yield purity instead of promiscuity.

THE DISCIPLINE OF COMPULSIVE SEXUAL PURITY

Although I believe the greatest problem for young people today is the broken family, each of these problems, in their own way, cause young people an omi-nous wave of emotion every day the sun rises and sets. But arguably, there is one issue looming over all of these others. We need an answer for the *compulsive sexual promiscuity* in society.

The free sexual practices of America have been shared and researched extensively.

We need a new *scriptural* pattern or disciplined practice of sexual morality to fight against the *cultural* pattern or practice of sexual immorality. We need an overwhelming *compulsive sexual purity* to rise up against the *compulsive sexual promiscuity* that exists in our world. A disciplined compulsion of the spiritual sexual disciplines in this chapter, lived out in the lives of our teenagers, will stand as a strong force against the onslaught of the sexual promiscuity in our society. Our teenagers' first response to the temptations in this world should be a compulsive sexual discipline to not give in.

FROM THE RISE IN ORAL SEX AMONG TEENS, THE MOVE TOWARD AN ACCEPTANCE OF BESTIALITY, THE CREATION OF SEXBOTS, AND THE UNTHINKABLE PUSH FOR LEGALIZED INCEST, WE NEED ANOTHER TSUNAMI TO CRASH ON THE SHORES OF OUR COUNTRY.

For example, the Bible states that God created male and female, and all of history has supported this, but the main reason we have had such a sweeping change in society's concept of sexuality is because we have had sweeping generational biblical loss in the last twenty-five years. This loss was caused by things like progressive education, lack of conservative censorship in the media, an entertainment industry pushing the envelope of progressive ideology, and systematic humanistic and postmodern breakaway from the Scriptures.

In the face of this sweeping sexual promiscuity, we need a recommitment to sexual purity, another tsunami to crash on the shores of America and wash away the debris left behind by current sexual revolution.

When we teach teenagers sexual discipline, it restores the original intent of the biblical worldview in their mind and ultimately in their world. It all starts one classroom at a time, one media post at a time, and one conversation at a time.

The more we know God in His completeness, the more assured I am that this generation will serve Him. Because if they *seek* Him, they will *see* Him, and if they *see* Him, they will *serve* Him. We must introduce Christ to this generation and watch them draw near to Him. We will witness a return to a compulsive sexual purity and the biblical ethic, and a generational run away from compulsive sexual promiscuity. *Because an undisciplined mind is the enemy of truth.*

OUR TEENAGERS' FIRST RESPONSE TO THE TEMPTATIONS IN THIS WORLD SHOULD BE A COMPULSIVE SEXUAL DISCIPLINE TO NOT GIVE IN.

FINALLY

The journey of a thousand miles begins with one step—one finally placed, disciplined step in the right direction.

We may have a long way to go in order to get our society back to sexual purity, but we are never closer than when we take the first step in the right direction.

Teenagers must settle their response to the sexual revolution *before* it shows up at their doorstep, before their peers start badgering them to have sex. Sexual sin is completely avoidable when we teach young people the principles in this chapter. When the *principle* of Christ as first or at the center of our life is a priority, we have all the power we need to stand against sexual temptation. Couple that with *practices* that protect our principles, and we become a force against the sexual revolution in this world.

We cannot lose sexual discipline and purity at the center of our lives. One of the main responsibilities of youth leaders is to prepare students to stand against the temptation in this world with the full armor of God so that they can withstand the enemy's tactics against them. This is done by giving teenagers and young people a complete sexual discipline. When the church fails to do that, our youth are led by social movements, not spiritual ones. What we desperately need today is another spiritual revolution in the young people of America to come up fiercely beside the current sexual revolution with truth and love!

My prayer for the sexual revolution moment we are in right now is that our faith will be tested—and shown to be real. *My prayer* is that we will raise a generation of teenagers who understand the complete theology of God so the testing of their faith will result in their faith being shared and spread, not stolen. *My prayer* is that a counterrevolution of sexual discipline will take place through a revival happening in the young people of the church, bringing about an awakening in their culture.

IF WE ARE GOING TO WIN A GENERATION, WE MUST HELP THEM SOLVE THE WORST OF THEIR PROBLEMS.

Revivals do not necessarily take place in culture; they take place in the church coming back to its life purpose. And when the church finds its purpose, an awakening takes place in culture as a result of the life being brought back into the church.

The sexual spiritual discipline of an entire generation could supersede the unbiblical viral concepts that were downloaded in our society in the last two decades. We need a countercultural download of conservative biblical ethics practiced by a generation and witnessed by a nation.

SMALL GROUP APPLICATION

Daniel Martinez, High School Pastor • Trinity Church, Cedar Hill, TX

What will it take to restore biblical sexuality? We live in a time of a sexual revolution in this generation and desperately need a counterrevolution of the Scriptures. There is an identity crisis, lack of priorities, no boundaries, no commitment to holiness, and a lack of a biblical worldview in teenagers and the home.

However, I have no doubt that we can restore sexuality to its purest form. The restoration of holiness must become a *priority* and not just a *proverb*. As you've seen in this book, we have to set practices to restore this generation to its original plan and purpose. It's no obligation; it's a decision of knowing who you are.

If we're going to restore sexuality, here's a practical place to start.

1. Know Your Identity

    » What does your name mean?

    » How does God see you?

    » Learn the sexuality design in Scriptures from: Genesis 1–3; the wisdom literature in the Psalms, Proverbs, and Song of Solomon; Matthew 5:27–32, 15:19; Romans 1:18–32; Galatians 5:16–24; 1 Corinthians 6–7; 1 Timothy 1:8–11; Jude 1; and Revelation 17–18.

2. Set Your Priorities

Write down and discuss the top five priorities in your life, and then ask yourself where sexuality is a priority of your life.

For example, God, family, school, sports, and friends all take up major thought patterns in a teenager's life.

Where is sexuality? How much time do you spend on biblical design and your identity? What are the practical guidelines in this chapter that will help protect your principles?

3. Safeguard Your Sexuality

Like the chapter says, we need practices that protect our principles. Every teenager should have safe practices they live by.

> » List five safe practices that you can implement into your life when it comes to your sexual purity.
> » Read Genesis 1–3 and 1 Corinthians 6–7. Talk about these verses and, as a group, come up with three conclusions.

4. Think About Holiness

God created us to be in a natural habitat of holiness—to be holy as He is holy. Just like we can't remove a fish from water and expect it to survive, we can't do the same with holiness as believers. It is our calling to be Christ-like.

> » What does holiness mean?
> » What does the Bible say about holiness? List three verses that deal with sexual purity.
> » What is an ethic?

5. Have a Plan and Stick to It

> » What is your dating "game plan"? Go over the *D.A.T.I.N.G.* acronym in this chapter.
> » What are your practical boundaries for your dating relationship?
> » What is your mate list? Create a list you have for yourself to help guide your choice of a boyfriend or girlfriend and, ultimately, your spouse. Write them down.

Daniel Martinez is the youth pastor for the Explicit Youth Ministry at Trinity Church in Cedar Hill, Texas. He and his wife Rachel and their team of youth pastors have a presence-based youth ministry that strives to place spiritual formation central to their philosophy of ministry on Wednesday nights, in their school outreach, and in a thriving fine arts program. They are providing the type of in-depth youth ministry we need in America.

SECTION TWO

THE OUTWARD DISCIPLINES

Healthy citizens are the greatest
asset any country can have.
—Winston Churchill

6

WELLNESS

(TOTAL HEALTH)

In what should be the best days of their lives, the teen years are becoming an adolescent nightmare.

When it comes to spiritual discipline, we don't often think of total wellness. But as young people created in the image of God, our temples are the body of the Lord. This places great responsibility on taking care of ourselves in all facets of life, including mental, physical, emotional, and relational health.

So let's take a look at the effect of total wellness and our mental health.

It is not lost on me that there are multiple issues that create poor mental health in teenagers. It could be a chemical imbalance in the physiology of a person, inadequate exercise and activity, poor family mental health history, image-based influence of social media, unrealistic peer comparison, a post-traumatic stress disorder, unbalanced dietary habits, or even the break-up of the family system. Whether separately or combined, all can cause mental health issues in teenagers. Whatever the cause of poor mental health, the reality is that we have seen a rise in depression—and, ultimately, suicide—in the Gen Z set, born around 1998 through 2013.

Additionally, the solutions for mental health issues could be as simple as better nutrition, adequate rest, recreation, and clinical counseling, or as exhaustive as medical prescriptions or admission to a mental health facility. Whatever it takes, there is no shame in working on your mental health. In fact, it has become increasingly popular for people to have counselors. I have seen a counselor every January or February for the past several years to help me with my mental health.

Mental health issues could spring from a variety of lifestyle patterns or changes, as well as chemical imbalances in a person's physiology. Whatever the cause, it will take a multifaceted approach to solve the mental health crises we have today among young people.

What must be addressed quickly is the adolescent mental health crisis spurred on by the COVID-19 virus and the resulting radical lockdowns and procedures. For example, we have spent the last two years insisting that science says our students should not socialize in community with their friends—at a time in their lives when socialization is fundamental to their personal growth and mental health.

And here is the outcome. According to a recent study by the World Health Organization (WHO) and the Allstate Foundation:

- A rising number of students feel uncertain, nervous, and stressed about the present school situation in America

- Before COVID-19, only 19 percent of the patients treated at mental health facilities were adolescents. Since COVID-19, that number has risen to 39 percent.

- Suicide is now the third leading cause of death among ages fifteen through nineteen.

GEN Z'S CURRENT STATE OF MENTAL HEALTH

During the lockdowns and mask mandates of 2020 and 2021, governors across the United States determined that closing government-run schools was in the best interests of American students. In some cases, governors demanded the closure of privately-run schools as well. These kind of decisions to enact national lockdowns created more health issues than the pandemic itself and must be reconsidered and revisited moving forward.

From New York to California, from Minnesota to Texas, public health officials, teachers' unions, and political activists have pressured politicians to act without due process to safeguard our children from COVID-19. As a college professor and youth development specialist of four decades, I am concerned by the effect of the rush of lockdown demands and the limited forethought these groups use in setting up safeguards to keep our students in school and social settings while considering health safety.

In response to these decisions, we must push back against Washington elites creating the national lockdowns and place these decisions into the hands of local officials. Because we did not adequately revisit these lockdown policies, the mounting mental and economic health of our children and families continues to be ignored. Poor mental health outcomes have become a worse problem than the COVID-19 pandemic itself. The rise in mental health issues among teenagers is extremely troubling. The teen years, which should be the best days of a young person's life, are becoming an adolescent nightmare.

THE RISE IN MENTAL HEALTH ISSUES AMONG TEENAGERS IS EXTREMELY TROUBLING. THE TEEN YEARS ARE BECOMING AN ADOLESCENT NIGHTMARE.

Why the overemphasis upon the physical health of our students and the complete lack of concern for their mental and emotional harm? Surely we could balance our efforts and come up with better solutions to mental health issues rather than focusing most of our attention on the physical health of our children.

THE POWER IN COMMUNITY

As humans, we were made to be with each other. Something special happens between people when they interact with one another in community. So a withdrawal from friends and regular events like school, sports, jobs, and faith-based activities that bring personal formation to teens is catastrophic. Without this crucial interaction during puberty and the adolescent formative years, long-term damage can be devastating to one's self-esteem, social interaction, and mental awareness.

Through all of these political decisions, we have also seen a devastating loss of social development with the closing of shopping malls, movies theaters, and sporting events for athletes and fans. COVID-19 lockdowns caused isolation and forced teenagers to be alone for extended periods of time. This isolation, coupled with poor self-esteem, has caused stress, loneliness, self-harm, eating disorders, problems in the family, and the removal of peer influence to help with critical thought, problem-solving, and dialogue.

In the wake of these political decisions and national lockdowns, the discontinuation of in-person learning left parents at home without access to the kind of teaching resources it takes to homeschool. We asked parents to pick up the pieces of cancelled graduation ceremonies, loss of college scholarship opportunities, terminated lunch services, and the loss of placement services for graduating students. And we are now living with the outcomes of isolation and a lack of community.

As a parent, educator, coach, or youth leader, identifying students who are struggling is not always easy. Although poor academic performance is not the only indicator, we must pay attention to the loss of education and graded measurements and standardization of students, the impacts of the discontinuation of terminology, content, and vocabulary, digital fatigue from exhaustive online formats, and the loss of daily routines to simply wake up, eat, and exercise.

THE DISCIPLINE OF WORDS AND MENTAL HEALTH

It will take a disciplined and strategic plan to reset the mental health of teenagers. One of the practices that will be important in doing so is the speaking of declarations over our lives. Our words are seeds that become planted in our heart and mind, taking root and growing into actions over time. What are you speaking over your life and the life of your family?

OUR WORDS ARE SEEDS THAT BECOME PLANTED IN OUR HEART AND MIND, TAKING ROOT AND GROWING INTO ACTIONS OVER TIME. WHAT ARE YOU SPEAKING OVER YOUR LIFE?

We have a practice in our home of speaking declarations over our children and grandchildren every single day. These declarations become a default framework to our thinking and really do shape our thoughts. When it comes to the discipline of mental health, there may not be a more powerful way for teenagers to battle against the negative thoughts of the mind. Use the following declarations, or create your own, to speak over your family every single day. There is a scriptural basis for all of these:

- You can do all things because God is your strength.

- You overcome evil with good.

- You keep your promises, and your yes is yes and your no is no.

- You feel all of your feelings and discharge them safely and completely.

- You make choices based on the truth of God's Word and not your feelings.

- You will love your wife just as Christ loves the church.

- You will submit to your husband as unto the Lord.

- You forgive because God has forgiven you.

- You have the mind of Christ and the wisdom of God.

- You are responsible for your own thoughts, feelings, attitudes, and actions. You are not responsible for or hindered by the thoughts, feelings, attitudes, and actions of others.

- You speak life and not death, blessings and not curses.

- You have God so you have all that you need.

- The joy of the Lord is your strength.

- The peace of God rules in your heart.

- You act justly, love mercy, and walk humbly.

- You give more than you take.

- You are thankful always.

- You are filled with the Holy Spirit.

- You resist the devil, and he will flee from you.

- You chase after what is pure.

- You know the difference between right and wrong, and you choose right every time.

- You are quick to repent when you make bad choices.

- You are a leader.

- You are not a quitter.

- Your identity, value, worth, and significance are in God alone, not in other people's approval or expectations, your appearance, possessions, productivity, performance, knowledge, or relationships.

Do you see the power in these declarations? You can memorize these as a family, print them out to post in your home, hang them on the mirror of your car, and speak them over your family daily.

The state of our teenagers' mental health is at crisis levels. This declining condition must be reversed with a greater and more focused emphasis upon mental health and total wellness. Fortunately, it is the powerful influence of words that can aid in shaping healthy minds in our young people.

THE POWER OF "ONE ANOTHER" AND WELLNESS

The Bible is filled with *"one another"* verses that define the importance of social interaction and the purpose for human community. I understand what people mean when they say things like, "I only need Jesus," or "Jesus is all I need." Sure, we are complete in Him, and Christ is all. But even Jesus Himself said that we need each other.

Look at the following Scripture passages that call us to the discipline of community and the personal health it produces:

In Judges 20:20–21, there is a story about the Israelites fighting in Gibeah against the tribe of Benjamin and losing 22,000 troops in one day. A devastating loss. But the next day, they did something that was nation-changing. Look at the next two verses:

> But the people, the men of Israel, took courage, and again formed the battle line in the same place where they had formed it on the first day. And the people of Israel went up and wept before the LORD until the evening.
>
> (Judges 20:22–23)

If you read the story, you will see that the Israelites lost again on the next day, but continued in their battle, and on the third day, they won a greater victory than they lost the previous two days. All because of the power of *one another*. It's a remarkable story of resilience and relationship and its effect upon us when we work together.

Here are some more verses about the impact of our relationships upon discipleship and spiritual formation. We cannot deny the power of one another in Christianity:

> As iron sharpens iron, so one person sharpens another.
>
> (Proverbs 27:17 NIV)

> No longer shall each one teach his neighbor and each his brother, saying, "Know the LORD," for they shall all know me.　　(Jeremiah 31:34)

> Do we not all have one Father? Did not one God create us? Why do we profane the covenant of our ancestors by being unfaithful to one another?
>
> (Malachi 2:10 NIV)

> A new commandment I give to you, that you love one another.
>
> (John 13:34)

> Be devoted to one another in love. Honor one another above yourselves.
>
> (Romans 12:10 NIV)

> Bear one another's burdens.　　(Galatians 6:2)

In your relationships with one another, have the same mindset as Christ Jesus.   (Philippians 2:5 NIV)

Let the word of Christ dwell in you richly, teaching and admonishing one another in all wisdom, singing psalms and hymns and spiritual songs.
(Colossians 3:16)

Encourage one another and build one another up.   (1 Thessalonians 5:11)

Stir up one another to love and good works, not neglecting to meet together.   (Hebrews 10:24–25)

Show hospitality to one another without grumbling.   (1 Peter 4:9)

You who are younger, submit yourselves to your elders.   (1 Peter 5:5 NIV)

There are many more great texts about the responsibility of discipleship and the discipline of mentoring and interpersonal relationship. I'm not sure we have discovered the value of relationship in the kingdom of God. Unfortunately, I have seen far too often that it is much easier for us to rejoice when someone has fallen, or celebrate the failure of someone else thinking that it will somehow benefit our well-being.

The church is defined as a family for many reasons. Look at the language of Scripture and the value it places on community and belonging.

THE DISCIPLINE OF FOLLOWING IS A FOUNDATIONAL
CORE VALUE IN THE KINGDOM OF GOD,
AND IT COULD BE KEY TO HEALING TO THE MENTAL
HEALTH ISSUES OF TEENAGERS.

It really is true that we need each other. Relationship is vital to mental health and discipleship.

TWO MAJOR CONCERNS FOR GEN Z

Let me offer two major concerns among Gen Z that have been the cause of many mental health problems and point to the need for elementary disciplines in an adolescent's life:

1. A SOCIALIZATION GAP

We were made to be with each other. Something special happens in community and interaction.

What is a socialization gap? Here are a few simple definitions:

- When a community restricts interpersonal networking and relational activities that create scenarios of learning in a social setting
- A withdrawal of someone from friends and weekly community interaction at school
- The cancellation of activities in a teen's life such as athletic teams, jobs, and concerts, dances, or other events
- The restriction of youth group and other faith-based programming in the local church that normally enhances personal formation for teens
- Closing of shopping malls, movie theaters, skating rinks, and other venues, creating a devastating loss of social development among teens

When social settings are limited, there is a lack of human development and fewer opportunities to learn from others.

These restrictions have caused isolation and forced teenagers and young people to be alone at a time when intersocial connection is so important. This isolation, coupled with poor self-esteem, has caused mental health stress, loneliness, self-harm, eating disorders, and problems in the family.

Of course, the COVID-19 lockdowns of 2020–2021 were a major factor in the loss of social disciplines. Unfortunately, Gen Z and now Alpha Gen may hear that they were *the pandemic generation*. I do not believe that and will never define them in this way.

One of the most important disciplines in adolescent life is community. Building relationships and interacting with groups of friends are skills we need to master as a child and teenager. When the socialization circles of our young people are limited—or, worse, taken away completely—our children lose important life stage development of their critical thinking skills, problem-solving approaches, and their confidence in interpersonal dialogue and conversation.

A second major mental health concern is the loss of the discipline of interaction and learning that takes place in the educational setting. Look at the importance of graded educational discipline and scholastic achievement.

2. AN EDUCATION GAP

We must close the educational gap in the lives of our young people. As a parent, educator, coach, or youth leader, identifying students who are struggling with education is not always easy. But here are a few research points on the educational development of teenagers in America over the last two years:

- Poor academic performance in school, loss of standardization, little tactile or group learning, discontinuation of graded content and vocabulary

- A loss of daily routines such as a waking, eating, or exercise schedule, loss of seated educational advantages, and digital fatigue from being online so much

- The discontinuation of education leaving parents at home without teaching resources, cancelled graduation ceremonies for seniors, lost college scholarship opportunities to scholars and athletes, stopped lunch services for students from the school system, and taking away placement services for graduating students

On top of the research statistics and this educational framework gap, look at the added stress of paying for college. If students do not make college preparation a priority, they will lose out in a competitive scholarship environment right now. And this could be a critical loss of opportunity for continuing education. All of these stressors have added up over the last two years and compounded the mental health issues of teenagers and adolescents.

Similar to the need for *socialization*—but even more critical because of the loss of language, terms, and content—is the need for the *educational* and scholastic growth of our children. I read a research article a few years ago about the adolescent education and self-esteem of the top ten countries in the world. It was a remarkable read on the reversal of the two data points in the survey with the United States.

THE NUMBER ONE COUNTRY IN THE WORLD FOR SELF-ESTEEM WAS TEENAGERS IN THE U.S. BUT THEY WERE NUMBER TEN IN EDUCATION GLOBALLY. THAT'S A PRETTY TELLING STATEMENT ABOUT THE CONFIDENCE OF A U.S. STUDENT WHO IS COMPARATIVELY IGNORANT GLOBALLY!

KEY ISSUES

To close out this chapter, let me give you some practical discipline about key issues in an adolescent's life.

DEPRESSION AND SUICIDE

Given these two major mental health concerns, let's look at how to stop the nightmare of depression or suicide in a teenager's life.

1. When talking to teens, compliments and encouragement go a long way. Use positive and uplifting words with teenagers because they are hearing a lot of negativity in their world. Again, our words are formative in a teenager's mind.

2. Bedtime routines can be a great way to fight against stress that leads to compounded mental health problems. Here are some practical ideas teens can use to counter depression:

- Before bed, avoid stressful mental activity and caffeine so you can get the rest you need

- Listen to worship music that will bring the presence of God into your room before bed

- Have an enjoyable, stress-free conversation with a friend

- Write a list of things need to be done so that you can get them off your mind

- Spend a few minutes reading Scripture

3. Youth leaders can help students find their purpose in life. The effect of a student understanding their purpose and design in life is a powerful influence on their psyche. There may be no better solution to depression and ultimately suicidal thoughts than a teenager discovering their purpose in life.

4. Encouraging students to see a counselor is an important step in completing a teen's efforts in total mental health. Be willing to set up the appointment, drive them to the appointment, and attend if needed.

Apply these few simple steps as a parent or leader over teenagers, and you will see marked improvement in their lives. Or, if you are a teenager, apply these to your own life, and watch your mental health improve in the area of stress, depression, or suicidal thoughts. It really does only take a few small things to change your thoughts and ultimately your life.

HEALTH AND WELLNESS

We must emphasize the importance of total wellness in the teenagers around us. Life disciplines such as eating a balanced diet, exercise, getting enough sleep, a walk outdoors, or focusing on how we manage our relationships are all a part of our total health and wellness. The proper regime contributes to balanced physiology in teenagers and ultimately contributes to positive mental health.

The restoration that takes place in recreation will change the physical health of your body at any age. Even minimal recreation practiced consistently will yield maximal return. Try these important practices and see if you feel better in one month:

- A daily, fifteen-minute recreation, such as walking, stepping, exercise, or stretching. Throughout the day, small amounts of recreation are especially helpful for ensuring good health.

- After workouts, try a warm bath with Epsom salt, which is rich in magnesium and helps to relax the muscles and the nervous system.

- Chamomile tea promotes relaxation as you unwind for a night of sleep.

- Aromatherapy minerals or spray can help to relieve any momentary feelings of grogginess.

- Bring conflict resolution to your relationships as soon as you are able to so that there is little lingering social stress in your life.

It may seem trivial, but total health and wellness is comprehensive discipline that yields long-lasting results in many areas of a young person's life.

PHYSICAL EXERTION HELPS YOUR BODY
BREAK DOWN AND SECRETE HARMFUL FLUIDS.
SOMETHING AS SIMPLE AS TAKING THE STAIRS RATHER
THAN THE ELEVATOR OR WALKING DURING YOUR
LUNCH BREAK CAN BE BENEFICIAL.

EMOTIONAL INTELLIGENCE (EI)

Emotional intelligence and brain health can be improved. A positive outlook is a powerful outcome. Changing our thought patterns will change our language, create better self-awareness and respect for others, put an end to bullying, and help teenagers do critical thinking instead of thinking critical thoughts. What a difference! If we can teach our young people to do strategic critical thinking, they will not get caught up in critical thoughts about everything in life.

EI can be a game changer in a young person's life. And it really doesn't take that much work. The emotional health of a person is maximized through a few routine practices:

- EI is developed with a mindset of resilience in the face of hardship or difficulty
- Optimism and a positive attitude give strength to our mind, body, and spirit
- Healthy, accountable friendships must become a priority in a teen's life
- Taking care of your physical person is a huge assist to your mental health
- Exercise and recreation create the full body workout that resets our body and cleanses it of unhealthy impurities and tension

FAITH

Maybe one of the lesser emphasized emotional intelligencers is our faith. Our faith has a powerful effect upon our emotions. I love the Proverbs' focus upon our thoughts, attitudes, and words to shape our mindset. For example, Proverbs 21:23 says, *"Whoever keeps his mouth and his tongue keeps himself out of trouble."*

Hebrews 11 is one of the best reads in all of the Scriptures. It reviews the people of Christianity throughout the ages, from Abraham to Christ and the disciples. The chapter tells of the signs, wonders, and miracles that accompany the great men and women of Christian history. And the recurring trait of these great leaders was faith. Over a dozen times, Hebrews 11 mentions the characteristic trait of faith that each of these people displayed.

Our wellness depends greatly on our faith. Faith is inspirational and calming. Faith is the common denominator of the saints who finished the course set before them. Here are a few practical ways to build your faith that will in turn influence your mental health:

- Praying regularly, reading the Bible, and worshipping God
- Practicing the spiritual disciplines daily
- Spending time with people of faith
- Obeying God's calling on your life
- Praying in the Spirit

THE FAMILY IMPACT ON MENTAL HEALTH

We are not just raising a fatherless generation anymore. We are raising a fatherless, motherless, and sibling-less generation. The family structure has been disintegrated in our country. And when the home is broken, society is broken.

There are so many positive ways that family can influence the mental health of our teenagers. To be honest, the most formative moments in a teenager's life occur in the home. It might be family dinners, game nights, recreation, or having friends over for sleepovers. Whatever the activity, it only takes a little effort to improve a teen's mental health. A safe place like home will allow teenagers to be comfortable with their wins and failures in front of people who love them unconditionally.

IN HIS FAREWELL ADDRESS TO THE NATION IN
JANUARY 1989, PRESIDENT RONALD REAGAN SAID,
"ALL GREAT CHANGE IN AMERICA BEGINS
AT THE DINNER TABLE."

Every society is built upon the health or the unhealth of the discipline of its families. This is the reason for the family being the segment of society to which we must place most of our focus in order to see total wellness in our children and ultimately our future. The family may not seem like a discipline, but the impact of the home on the total wellness of our children cannot be overstated.

Here are a few things to keep in mind as we look at the impact of family on mental health:

- Our families and homes are the incubator of healthy children.
- The sibling relationship may be one of the most important disciplines we teach our young people early in life.
- The family is the best contextual way to speak the language of the communities in which they live.

- Our families are at the core of our community life.

- The presence of the family is the one system that exists in every community globally.

- When a family resides in a community, they have immediate access to adapt to its ecosystem.

- Missiology is the study of intention and mission in a certain place. What better way to be missional than to use families to reach families with the gospel?

- Adults and children build relationships and cross the multigenerational divide.

- The only cost to this kind of mental health is the cost of the discipleship of our children.

HEALTHY MARRIAGES AND PARENTING

The parents in a home model honor, respect, communication, and authority. When the marriage and the parenting relationship is healthy, the family will also be healthy. Maybe you are in a traditional home with both biological parents present, a blended home, or even a home with a single parent. There is no default home in America.

Raising healthy young adults begins at home in our families. Mental health and total wellness is comprehensive yet easily applied in our family relationships. I have often watched the best kids come from the worst homes, and the worst kids come from the best homes. It is a matter of parental leadership and authority. Build a loving and accepting space that your children will want to run home to!

THE FAMILY TABLE

What a place of impact! When the family creates a meal together, magic happens. This discipline should occur at least two or three times a week. The conversations that take place around the table will change your family dynamic.

We always had a rule in our home that you *can* talk with food in your mouth! This is the place where everyone finds out how everyone else is doing. A family conversation around the table important for building relationships, identity, and trust.

SIBLING RELATIONSHIPS

We have lost the sibling relationship in our homes over the last twenty-five years. I can remember growing up with my brothers and sister, and the impact they had on my life. Siblings have a special way of benefiting us through conversation, accountability, and understanding.

The sibling relationship is truly one of the most healthy and protective unions between human beings. Our families can build healthy relationships with each other by holding family meetings and having siblings pick each other up from events, help with homework or chores, go for walks, cook a meal together, and other bonding activities.

FAMILY RECREATION

When is the last time you had a family vacation? My children still talk about vacations that we took years ago. Every family could use more memories, laughter, and education. Family vacations can create all of these things. The inspiration that comes from family recreation can also take place with movie nights, board games, and yard games that cost very little or nothing.

Maybe you need to get creative and have a staycation in your area that lasts the weekend and doesn't cost that much. Or maybe you could plan a day trip to a museum or a park. My son, who lives in Los Angeles, takes his three kids to get doughnuts every Saturday morning! Something tells me they will never forget this.

COMMUNITY INVOLVEMENT

Community involvement is a great discipline in the home. Maybe you go to a local shelter or a food kitchen to help serve the homeless. Or maybe you volunteer at a local nonprofit. There are all kinds of ways for a family to be present in the community where they live.

Our family committed to providing meals at Thanksgiving. We would go to the grocery store and let the kids choose the groceries and then deliver them to a family in need. Another great way to have an impact on the community is to be involved with the activities and events in your area. Sports teams, fine arts programs, or club involvement are easy to attend because our children are involved already. Try getting involved with the local schools and meeting other parents, teachers, coaches, and even your neighbors.

THE SABBATH

The discipline of the Sabbath is discussed in chapter 11, but for now, I would like to point out how important the Sabbath is to total wellness. We need teens to slow down. Remember, the Sabbath is actually a commandment, not a suggestion. For rest to be in God's Top 10 list is a pretty big deal.

> *WE DON'T HAVE TO FILL OUR LIVES WITH PROGRAMMED EVENTS OR ACTIVITIES. THE REGENERATION THAT TAKES PLACE DURING A SABBATH IS TRANSFORMATIVE.*

We don't have to always fill our lives with programmed events or activities. Even having a night off once a month can provide stress relief. The regeneration that takes place during a Sabbath is transformative to total health development.

FINALLY

Our children's mental health is in a crisis. Instead of a teenager's life being a dream here in America, it has become a nightmare. If we are going to solve this, science and politicians across the country are going to have to see the devastating results of isolation and disorientation that comes from social distancing and its effect upon teenagers. And make changes.

Try using these preventative actions against depression and suicide in teenagers. You may be able to curb the downhill mental health spiral of a teenager in your life if you catch it quickly.

TEENAGERS AT RISK

It's essential for youth leaders to receive the education and development necessary to deal with crises in the life of an adolescent. When it comes to intervention and proximity, youth leaders must recognize basic competencies that will allow them to help teenagers when crisis enters their lives.

WHEN WE SPEAK WITH A SUICIDAL TEEN,
WE DRAW THEM TO HOPE BY COMMUNICATING WITH
THEM AND GETTING THEM TO TALK.
ASK QUESTIONS THAT SHOW YOU REALLY CARE.
THE MORE THEY TALK, THE BETTER.

HOPE DEALERS

A term taken from the late Seventies anti-drug culture, *hope dealers* is the perfect description for youth leaders who work with Gen Z and their wildly out of control culture.

Have you looked around at American life recently? This is not your grandmother's world anymore. We often portray our lives as idyllic, our homes as perfect castles fit for princes and princesses, kings and queens. But have we forgotten about the dragons and the jesters? Social media shows happy, fairytale photos, but the truth may be closer to a nightmare. It's not all about moats and steeples, gardens and banquets.

In reality, we are really broken. I see it all the time in America. Machismo says, "I'm okay, you're okay." Pop psychology cannot deal with the reality of the wave of crisis or hardship or suffering in our lives, so it denies that a problem exists.

SOCIAL MEDIA SHOWS HAPPY, FAIRY-TALE PHOTOS, BUT THE TRUTH MAY BE CLOSER TO A NIGHTMARE. IN REALITY, WE ARE REALLY BROKEN.

A BETTER VIEW OF HARDSHIP

What we need as youth leaders is a new perspective.

As youth leaders, we will have to respond often to a teenager who has been hit by all kinds of problems. The stories of teens whose lives were torn apart by hardship must be carefully put back together by skilled youth leaders with necessary coping skills and a whole lot of hope.

We must all be *hope dealers* to a generation that's buried by despair. Hope is something that I have used countless times in my work with young people. Just look at the kind of things that teenagers are growing up with:

- At-risk behaviors like self-harm, suicide, cutting, and bullying
- The broken family
- The sexual revolution
- A social media delusion
- Post-Christian society
- Violence in our schools
- A broken government and angry society

Given this environment in our society and the teen world, here are some practical responses to handling teens in crisis:

- *When we speak with a suicidal teen*, we draw them to hope by communicating with them and getting them to talk. Ask questions that show you really care about them. Ask about their family, their friends, their hobbies, or their work. The more they talk, the better. And this conversation will help you prevent their decision of harm and see if they are willing to hang out with you the next day. This will often not only delay the action, but stop it altogether.

- *When I speak with a young girl who is cutting and doing self-harm*, I draw her to hope by saying she is not the only one going through this. I love to tell the stories of other teens who were doing the same thing and stopped. Hearing that someone else has gone through or is going through the same thing lets them know they are not alone.

- *When we speak to a teenage boy living with a grandparent because his home is torn apart by divorce*, we have to find the positive in this situation. Try to get the teenager to see that a relationship with their grandparents is rare. Many young people never get this opportunity to stop the effects of dysfunction by being with their grandparents.

- *When we speak to teens about the condition of their world and society*, we must speak to them about leadership. The emphasis must be placed on being producers and not consumers of culture. It is innate in Gen Z to think and act as aspiring writers, publishers, and code-setters.

The role youth leaders play in raising disciples requires particular care regarding the total wellness of teenagers. Our focus on their total life care is critical to adolescent spiritual and social development. Our understanding of their world can make a difference and prevent them from becoming casualties to all kinds of at-risk crises.

But in order to do this, we must understand the kind of things that impact the world of a teenager—social circles, mental health, wellness, media, entertainment, education, government, and faith. And we must have the proximity and trust to be able to speak into their lives and give them the necessary leadership skills to not only cope, but to succeed, to become Christlike pioneers and pace-setters in this world, and kings and queens in the next.

SMALL GROUP APPLICATION

Will Ceaser, Youth Pastor • First Assembly of God, Dothan, AL

The greatest gift that you can give to your family, organization, or ministry is to be healthy. The Bible gives us a clear picture in what a completely healthy life looks like:

> *"And you shall love the Lord your God with all your heart* [emotionally] *and with all your soul* [spiritually] *and with all your mind* [mentally] *and with all your strength* [physically]*...You shall love your neighbor as yourself* [relationally]*." There is no other commandment greater than these.*
>
> (Mark 12:30–31)

Therefore, I'm motivated, convinced, and convicted that Christian teenagers should be the healthiest people in the world. So let's break down each aspect of our health.

First, *mental health matters*. It is important because you are what you think. (See Proverbs 23:7.) Your life goes in the direction of your strongest thoughts (see Proverbs 4:23), so if you want to change your life, you must let God change your mind.

> *Do not be conformed to this world, but be transformed by the renewal of your mind, that by testing you may discern what is the will of God, what is good and acceptable and perfect.* (Romans 12:2)

Ask yourself:

- What are two negative thoughts that keep coming up in your life?
- How can you overcome those thoughts and bring them under control?

Second, *place a high importance on presence and consistency*. If our physical health will not allow us to be physically present, we need to make sure that we change that. We cannot ask people to devote themselves to a life of discipline and devotion while excusing ourselves from it.

- Rate your physical health on a scale of one to ten, with one being unhealthy and ten being excellent health

- How could you improve your physical wellness?

Third, *develop emotional health to recognize and manage your emotions well.* We must control our behavior in response to other people's actions. Emotional quotient is the ability to identify, understand, and manage the emotions that you have. It's the ability to self-regulate.

- Talk about a time when your emotions got out of control. What did you learn?

- Talk about a time when you controlled your emotions. What did you learn from that moment?

Finally, *relational heath comes from relational intelligence.* This starts first with our love for God because only when we love God first can we love others better. Relational health is putting the right people in the right places to have the right life.

- Define your friends and their impact on your life.

- Define your impact on your friends' lives.

Will Ceaser serves as youth pastor at First Assembly of God in Dothan, Alabama, along with his wife, Lindsey. He has been in ministry for almost ten years. Youth First, the youth ministry at Dothan First, serves junior and senior high school students. Its vision is to see students devoted to Jesus Christ and His church through worship, learning God's Word, and a consistent prayer life.

We make a living by what we get, but we make a life by
what we give.
—Winston Churchill

7

GENEROSITY

(GIVING)

Teenagers and generosity?

Now, you may be thinking that teenagers and generosity—specifically money—do not go well together. You may think that they do not consider giving, that they are takers, too selfish, or perhaps broke. But that is simply not true. Well, they may be broke, but they know where to get the money. I'm sure all the parents know what I'm talking about.

What I have learned in almost four decades of youth ministry is that teenagers have grown up in a society that is consumer driven, and this setting has created adolescent consumer greed!

This chapter will not take on the task of talking about the giving of time and talents. We are going to stick to the discipline of money, giving, and generosity—specifically how to create *purposefully generous teenagers* when it comes to money. By the end of this chapter, I want to see teenagers and young people excited about the discipline of generosity, to help create purposefully generous teenagers where generosity is the principle, but giving is the practice.

> *TEENAGERS HAVE GROWN UP IN A SOCIETY THAT IS CONSUMER DRIVEN, WHICH HAS LED TO ADOLESCENT CONSUMER GREED.*

THE MERCHANTS OF COOL

Our culture has this generation wrapped around its slick marketing ploys. They have created consumers out of teenagers, who are the target of almost every marketing campaign for almost every Fortune 500 company. The problem with this is that *God has created us to be producers* and not merely consumers.

The marketing community and the advertising gurus in America have become the merchants of cool. They are business owners who spend millions of dollars to find out what is cool—popular, accepted, or trendy—and shape their product success through this data. There are about 32 million teenagers in America, and they command over $65 billion in disposable income. And with this wealth, they are exposed to over three thousand advertising messages in an average day. All of these merchants of cool are vying for a piece of the teenage pie!

THE MILLENNIALS AND GEN Z,
THE YOUNG ADULTS AND TEENS IN AMERICA RIGHT
NOW, HAVE BECOME THE TARGET OF THE
MERCHANTS OF COOL FOR 65 BILLION REASONS.

Unfortunately, compared to adults, teens respond to *cool* much simpler and faster. Because of this, whatever the trend-setters and merchants say is relevant becomes the newest need of the moment, which ultimately means profit for the *merchants*.

With this adolescent capital comes great responsibility to somehow help a generation purpose their finances and consumer power. I am praying for the greatest impact on our teen and young adult generation; I'm praying for their generosity and giving. Youth leaders in the marketplace and ministry settings have a significant role to play. We cannot underestimate the plan that God has for the young people of this generation to reach this planet with their wealth.

We must create the discipline of giving, benevolence, and generosity during the most important days in the lives of our youth. Look at these research findings:

- More than two-thirds of teens will leave their faith after high school. Why? Eighty-seven percent of the college kids surveyed said their friends led them away from the church.

- MSNBC boasted that Christian universities' policies of abstinence and the idea that "sex outside of marriage" is a sin or wrong is "not a very fun" experience for college students.

- Although eight out of ten teens say they are Christian, only two out of ten also claim to be "absolutely committed to the Christian faith."

- Just 16 percent of U.S. teens rank becoming spiritually mature as a future goal for their life.

- Only 50 percent of Christian teens read their Bible once a week.

- Thirty-one percent of Christian teens don't believe that forgiveness of sins is only possible through Jesus Christ.

Given the research, we must help to change the mindset of this generation; they must become arrows rather than targets. (See Psalm 127:4–5.) What a powerful thought—that teenagers can be on the offensive and not merely living on the defensive in this world. All of the data and research shows that one of the growing characteristic traits of Gen Z is that they are publishers and creators. We have a great responsibility to shape the young people of the twenty-first century to develop their creator mentality. They can be much more than mere spectators and consumers.

Given the Gen Z characteristic trait of publishing and creating, particularly online content, the change from *consumer* to *producer* should be an easy one. I'm not sure that there has ever been a time when young people could have a greater revolutionary impact upon their generation, our nation, and, ultimately, the world through both their consumer and producer traits.

Many factors—including our era of social media, the political unrest across the planet, the disintegration of the family, a loss of the sanctity of sexuality and identity, and the lack of spiritual passion—have led to a great sociological vacuum. For this generation to step up now would reform their world—and ours. It doesn't matter if you are a gym rat, brainiac, skater, alternative, rocker, shopper, or pastor's kid, God has a plan for your life at one of the most pivotal times in human history.

> **IF YOUNG PEOPLE REACH THEIR GOD-GIVEN DESIGN OF GENEROSITY AND GIVING, THEY COULD USE THEIR FINANCES AND WEALTH TO RID THE EARTH OF POVERTY, SICKNESS, AND STARVATION.**

The best way to put the merchants of cool out of business is to help young people reach their God-given design of generosity and giving. They could become so benevolent that their finances and wealth would be purposed to rid the earth of poverty, sickness, and starvation, rather than recklessly spending and hoarding stuff they don't need.

What can the church do? Help to create purposefully benevolent teenagers where generosity is the principle but giving is the practice.

FOR GOD SO LOVED..

Probably one of the most recognizable verses in the Bible tells us, *"For God so loved the world that He gave His only begotten Son, that whoever believes in Him should not perish but have everlasting life"* (John 3.16 NKJV).

Giving is one of the most important marks of Christianity. It is the crux of our faith as Christians. Faith, hope, and love come first, of course, but I would place *giving* in the next three most important words in Christianity, mostly because of this verse. God's actionable love was giving!

Many churches will do a series annually on tithing and generosity. This has made me think about the giving of this generation of young people. Teens spend about $65 billion in disposable income every year, proving that they are big-time consumers. I would like to see the church capitalize on this spending trend for the benefit of poverty, starvation, and mission, rather than selfish ambition and greedy gain.

WHAT DO TEENAGERS SPEND THEIR MONEY ON?
CLOTHING, CINEMA TICKETS, ALL KINDS OF MEDIA
MEMBERSHIPS, SPORTING EVENTS, CLOTHING,
COSMETICS, JEWELRY, ELECTRONICS, CLOTHING, AND
GAMING. OH, AND CLOTHING.

The lifestyle and creation of adolescent ego is extraordinary and requires expensive stuff. However, getting an adolescent to change their spending habits may be next to impossible without tapping into their God-given traits. The problem with this is that most of us have never outgrown the childish desire to take and to hold. When a child has a grip on their favorite toy, they cannot be separated from it very easily. You are in for a battle. In the same way, when a teenager has their mind set on a game, an article of clothing, or a concert ticket, it's difficult to talk them out of that desire. Letting go is not easy.

TEENAGERS AND TITHING

This makes me think of the biblical expectation of giving and the tithe, the biblical principle of giving 10 percent of our income back to the Lord. I'm not going to defend tithing here because it is biblically sound. When we do the work of looking at finances and the Bible, we realize the austerity of giving and God allowing us to keep 90 percent of our income. What a deal!

To look at giving from the Old Testament tithing perspective is quite easy and painless. On the other hand, the New Testament concept of giving is shocking. Jesus said we must give up everything, not just the classic 10 percent. (See, for example, Matthew 19:21; Mark 10:21; Luke 14:33.) But I'm sure we don't want to have a discussion about giving everything. So maybe we should just stick to the 10 percent! That's a much better deal.

A quick glance at the numbers shows that as a church, we haven't been obedient to the tithe and generosity. We are more apt to spend than to save, and we tend to consume more than we produce. Unfortunately, the generosity of adults has not set the best principle of generosity for the next generation, especially as it relates to giving of finances to the church.

According to research from multiple sources:

- There are about 32 million teenagers in America, and they have an expendable income of about $65 billion.
- The average teenager in America spends about $2,300 annually.
- Only about 5 percent of all churchgoers, 12 percent of evangelicals, and a little more than 30 percent of Pentecostals tithe.
- More than 80 percent of the world's wealth giving is done in North America.
- Thirty-six percent of American churches reported a decline in giving in 2020, up from 28 percent in 2019.
- The average American only gives between 1 and 3 percent of their income to any charity, but the average Christian gives 11 to 20 percent.
- Seventy-eight percent of churchgoers have given some amount of an offering at least once a month.

It is obvious that we have a lot to learn when it comes to the discipline of generosity.

GIVING EXPLOSION

Numbers like that can invoke a lot of opinion. What I want to focus upon is generosity. What would happen if the church gave the biblical command to tithe?

If believers were to increase their giving to a minimum of, let's say, 10 percent, there would be an additional $165 billion for churches to use and distribute just in the United States. The global impact would be phenomenal. Here's just a few things the church could do with that kind of money:

- $1 billion could fully fund all overseas mission work in the church
- $25 billion could relieve global hunger, starvation, and deaths from preventable diseases in five years
- $12 billion could eliminate illiteracy in five years
- $15 billion could solve the world's water and sanitation issues, specifically at places in the world where a billion people live on less than $1 per day
- $100 to $110 billion would still be left over for additional ministry expansion and taking care of the poor right here in our own country

When you look at tithing and giving, God really does have a great plan!

FOUR WAYS TO INVOLVE YOUTH

The reality is that our faith is generous. Generosity shows up foremost in the kind of faith we have. So how do we increase giving (and not just tithing) among the youth in our culture? Here are four ways to see our youth involved in greater giving and the discipline of generosity:

1. FOCUS ON THE PROBLEM

The real problem is not about money but about the heart. As Jesus said, *"For where your treasure is, there your heart will be also. The eye is the lamp of the body. So, if your eye is healthy, your whole body will be full of light, but if your eye is bad, your whole body will be full of darkness. If then the light in you is darkness, how great is the darkness!"* (Matthew 6:21–23).

We must deal with the heart first. If we win the heart, we win the wallets and the purses. The greatest key to change is to deal with the heart. Help students to see the need. If they see the problem or the need, they will help meet it because every sociological model has shown that teenagers are moved by a cause. It could be water wells in Africa, safe homes in Europe for victims of human trafficking, or crisis humanitarian work in the disaster relief zones globally.

Teaching our children to be givers to the needs of others starts early.

- Challenge them to give birthday money, Christmas money, or other cash gifts to a charity or mission
- Identify a family mission project and raise money each year for the cause
- Provide gifts, groceries, gas cards, or other expendable gifts to neighbors or others in need at Thanksgiving or Christmas

2. MODEL GIVING

As parents and youth leaders, we have to model giving in front of young people in our personal daily lives. When young people see us as givers, it will be easy for them to follow. Do they hear us talking about giving, paying for a meal when they are out with us, or even living on less and being content?

It is the responsibility of one generation to show the next generation the way to go. The reality is that about 87 percent of American teenagers' $65 billion in disposable income comes from their parents. So how can we teach parents and guardians to help their children make the right choices with their money?

- Give them an allowance for chores around the house or yard
- Establish a bank savings account when they are young and contribute to it with your change
- Encourage them to get a part-time job when they are able
- Allow your children to see you give the tithe and offerings

WE NEED TO USE THESE PRACTICAL PRINCIPLES
TO HELP CREATE PURPOSEFULLY GENEROUS
TEENAGERS WHERE GENEROSITY IS THE PRINCIPLE,
BUT GIVING IS THE PRACTICE.

We are only effective when we demonstrate that we tithe and give. We cannot expect our children to be givers if we ourselves are not givers. They will see it in our priorities. Do we talk about giving at home? Are we paying for lunches when another family goes out with us after church? Do we give in the offerings at church? Do we support missionaries? What about sponsoring a needy family during the holidays? All of these things add to the kind of discipline we have as parents and leaders in front of our children.

3. CHALLENGE YOUNG PEOPLE TO GIVE

We have under-challenged teenagers in the church. All across our nation, young people are giving to the church and its mission. In my denomination's Next Gen Ministries across the nation, we gave over $17.3 million! Think about that. There are about 300,000 teenagers in the Assemblies of God denomination in the U.S. That would mean the average teenager in our movement gave about $56 to missions. How much more could we give if we could simply doubled that to $100 per student?

In my experience, teenagers will rise to the occasion every time if they are challenged.

Here are some practical ideas for helping teenagers become disciplined in giving:

- Demonstrate a family model of giving and teaching
- Teach young people to give their birthday money to missions or a missionary
- Challenge teenagers to give their graduation money toward a personal mission trip before they go off to college
- Encourage teenagers to give their Christmas money to a specific cause or charity
- Promote purposeful giving in the youth service on a regular basis
- Share opportunities or causes to give to every year, such as a vehicle, home, boat, or donkey for a missionary family
- Teach annually on giving in the youth ministry
- Highlight a story about a teenager who is giving and watch that model encourage everyone else to do the same

If the expendable income is there, we must appeal to the teens holding that $65 billion. Creating a discipline takes repetition and pattern over time, something that each of these principles could do.

4. PRESENT A CAUSE

One thing I have learned about young people after years working with them is that they love a cause. Especially Gen Z now. They are all in for building wells, stopping human trafficking, and solving food poverty globally. When you can clearly define a need to youth, they will step up and do something about it. It might be money for chickens for a village in Africa or donated clothes for the homeless in their own community. But a clear need is a cleared need!

> ## WHEN YOU CAN CLEARLY DEFINE A NEED TO YOUTH, THEY WILL STEP UP AND DO SOMETHING ABOUT IT. A CLEAR NEED IS A CLEARED NEED!

It is true that the need could be met through their time and their talents, but the easiest way to make a difference is when teenagers give. Their heart will follow their giving! It's wonderful to see what happens when a teenager's heart is into something. Define the cause and teenagers will get in line.

5. TELL THE STORY

We all love a story. Find as many inspirational stories as you can, share these with a teenager, and watch them fall in love with giving. This principle is tied to their identity and need for making a change. As producers, they will step to the front of the line and make a difference.

We don't tell our stories in Christianity very well. We must celebrate wins better. It isn't humility to keep a cause or a good deed toward that cause hidden. I understand privacy and motive with our giving and tithing records, but I don't believe our motives are carnal when we publish His works through a teen's giving. It could also stir others to good deeds.

Telling of a teenager and their story of giving puts all of these practical ideas together into a highly motivational tool to show other teenagers that they can do the same thing. Create a monthly video or social media story with the giving of students and watch the multiplied result.

A SLAP, A SHIRT, AN EXTRA MILE

One of my favorite parts of the Sermon on the Mount, where Jesus is setting up the kingdom of God on earth, is from Matthew 5:38–42:

> *You have heard that it was said, "An eye for an eye and a tooth for a tooth." But I say to you, Do not resist the one who is evil. But if anyone slaps you on the right cheek, turn to him the other also. And if anyone would sue you and take your tunic, let him have your cloak as well. And if anyone forces you to go one mile, go with him two miles. Give to the one who begs from you, and do not refuse the one who would borrow from you.*

Within these words is a radical shift, a disciplinary financial revolution. The Sermon on the Mount is one of Jesus's most public discourses on the kingdom of God. He talked often about living different from the world, living in contrast to society. Look at Jesus's commands in this sermon like this:

- *The slap.* How can you turn the other cheek and be a peacemaker? What is going to be your generous response to the ill treatment you receive from the world? Return a slap with a smile.

- *The shirt.* What can you do to give more than expected? Instead of giving just a shirt, why not give a coat also? Think about rounding your giving up and not down.

- *The extra mile.* Are you willing to go out of your way? In the first century, a Roman soldier could compel any Jew to carry his load for one mile. Jesus said to do a little more.

Giving really is a revolutionary way to define the kingdom of God to those around us. Up until now, we have not demonstrated Christianity very well through the discipline of giving.

The Australian global church, Hillsong, produced a worldwide television event entitled *We're All in This Together* a few years ago. United Live, the youth worship movement from Hillsong Church, challenged the global church to greater action concerning giving, justice causes, and affecting our world for Christ.

One of the key statements in this production was the driving force behind the challenge of this documentary: *"When we forsake the needs of others, we actually forsake ourselves."* This moving statement actually underscores the meaning behind Jesus's words in Matthew 5.

Look for an opportunity to place others in front of yourself today. The kingdom of God is in the heart of every believer. What does that look like? According to Jesus, it looks like turning your cheek from the slap, giving your shirt to a friend, and being willing to do a little extra.

THE GOAL OF THIS CHAPTER IS TO
HELP CREATE PURPOSEFULLY GENEROUS
TEENAGERS WHERE GENEROSITY IS THE PRINCIPLE,
BUT GIVING IS THE PRACTICE.

FINALLY

Young people will be able to command a kingdom's ransom of millions of dollars when they have learned to command their own personal wealth with purpose and intention. When they have disciplined their finances and been obedient to the tithe and stewardship of what God has given them, they will in turn impact a far greater revolution in their generation—a revolution of generosity.

One of the most important lessons in my life came in a simple statement by Wayne Benson, the lead pastor who shaped my life and ministry when I began in ministry almost forty years ago. He said, "Jeff, never forget that you are paid from the tithe of a single mother who is trying to make her ends meet, from a college student who is in debt and works two jobs, and from an elderly couple who is giving from their retirement check."

I've never forgotten those words. They seeded the principle of stewardship and austerity in me. Those words have guided me when I'm shopping, eating out, or paying my bills. I wish those words would ring in the ears of everyone who reads this book because they were life-changing words for me to hear as a young youth pastor in the most formative years of my life.

Remember that American teenagers' disposable income totals about $65 billion *every year*. If we fail to teach, model, and create generosity in our teens, we fail to direct that money to advance God's kingdom.

IF WE FAIL TO TEACH, MODEL, AND CREATE GENEROSITY IN OUR TEENS, THEY WILL NOT USE THEIR $65 BILLION IN ANNUAL DISPOSABLE INCOME TO ADVANCE GOD'S KINGDOM.

Because giving and generosity are not something that comes naturally to humankind, we have to start somewhere. Starting with our young people seems the best way to impact the vacuum of giving that exists in adults.

The sustainability of the church depends upon the generosity of teenagers and young adults who will become the next leaders of the mission of the church. Young people will become the next financiers of the church. Maybe these practical ideas will help your teenagers become investors and not just consumers. Let's help our young people build a life defined by what they give and not by what they take.

SMALL GROUP APPLICATION

Lulu Murphy, Youth Pastor • River Valley Church, Apple Valley, MN

Generosity. How do we begin to unpack such a controversial topic like giving? And, specifically, how do we talk about money?

What I have learned in youth ministry is that students have money. The important part of our work with young people is how to teach them what to do with their money. How do we teach young people to manage their money and feel convicted to be generous with what's in their hands?

I share the story of the widow's offering often with students and leaders because it perfectly narrates what it looks like to live a life that's marked with radical generosity.

> *Sitting across from the offering box, he was observing how the crowd tossed money in for the collection. Many of the rich were making large contributions. One poor widow came up and put in two small coins—a measly two cents. Jesus called his disciples over and said, "The truth is that this poor widow gave more to the collection than all the others put together. All the others gave what they'll never miss; she gave extravagantly what she couldn't afford—she gave her all."* (Mark 12:41–44 MSG)

I love what it says at the end there. *"She gave her all."* While in giving the total amount, she did not give the most by any means, but she still gave out of a belief that we should all be living with—that she didn't *have to* give, but she *got to* give. I think it's very easy to say that we give regularly to this cause, or I support a certain missionary, but is it out of an obligation or a heart posture? As Jeff stated in this chapter, generosity is the principle, but giving is the practice. And it begins first in our hearts, not when we enter an amount.

The discipline of generosity begins when we have the revelation that God so loved the world that He *gave* His one and only Son. (See John 3:16.) This is the gospel; we are to *give*. The gospel message starts with generosity. Think of that. Being generous not only marks our lives as Christ followers, but it's also a privilege because it makes us more like Jesus.

GENEROSITY OUTLINE

After reading Mark 12:41-44, ask the group the following questions:

- Are you giving your *all* when it comes to being generous? Why or why not?

  » What does *giving your all* mean to you?

  » What have you given lately? Anything?

- Are you living this Scripture out?

  » How are you currently being generous in your life?

  » What are some ways that you feel convicted about being more generous in your life?

- Ask your youth pastor or youth leader, "What are some causes that our youth group gives to?"

  » If there isn't currently one, you take the initiative and find an organization or nonprofit that you feel passionate about raising money for. Start something with your friends to make an impact in building God's kingdom around the world.

  » Here are some example organizations to give to just to get you started: Speed the Light, World Serve, Venture, and Live Dead.

- Who are the most generous people you know? Ask them questions about how they live out a life of generosity every day.

Give yourself a goal. I want to give _____ to _____ organization or church youth group by this date: _____. I don't know about you, but I am pretty competitive, so having a goal in mind always helps me to want to cross the finish line and achieve it!

Lulu Murphy is youth pastor at River Valley Church in Apple Valley, Minnesota. She is part of the student ministry team that raises over $500,000 for missions annually. The culture of giving stems from the generosity of their lead pastor, who has guided the whole church to give more than $11 million to missions annually. Lulu studied family social science at the University of Minnesota, Twin Cities.

Start where you are. Use what you have. Do what you can.
—Arthur Ashe

8

ADMINISTRATION

(ORGANIZATION)

Sometimes the reason why our lives are all mixed up is because we didn't take the time to simply organize a few things—like maybe our calendar, our locker, our homework, and of course, our bedroom. I see administration and organization as simplicity.

I have learned that one of the hardest parts of discipline and leadership is self-discipline and self-leadership. Leading myself is much more difficult than leading others, running my ministry, or managing my organization. This gift of administration and organization simplifies every area of our lives.

I know administration and organization are not sexy or popular topics to talk about when it comes to spiritual disciplines. And most people may not even see the value of administration and organization as a spiritual gift. But the Scriptures are clear in Romans 12:7–8 and 1 Corinthians 12:28 that administration is one of the spiritual gifts the Holy Spirit gives us. Paul also lays out the argument for the importance of this gift in Colossians when he says, *"Whatever you do, in word or deed, do everything in the name of the Lord Jesus, giving thanks to God the Father through him"* (Colossians 3:17).

The concept of organization is seen throughout Scripture, so let's help teenagers in this spiritual discipline of the gift of administration.

What is the relationship between preparation and providence or success? Is there a connection between administration and blessing? What is the relationship between grit and opportunity?

In any organizational endeavor, there will always be the balance of hard work and luck! Some people are organizational gurus who create systems for high achievement. Others are relational gurus who create the environment for high achievement. The best teams and organizations will have both.

And then, what about God as the providential presence who makes it all happen as He wishes? We need all of these efforts working in our personal life and within any organization. We need the structure, the preparation, proven systems, simplicity, the work ethic, resources, creativity, relational community, and ultimately, the providential blessing.

THE GIFT OF ADMINISTRATION

God has given us all kinds of gifts to help us be successful in our spiritual life, including faith, mercy, encouragement, miracles, healing, prophecy, hospitality, discernment, and administration. One of the most important concepts that I would like you to consider is that administration is a gift. It can be given to us. Some spiritual gifts can grow, but generally, they are given to us, and we can use them without experience.

Administration is the organizational gift of the Spirit. A broad assist to our lives, it can be seen in the areas of systems, schedules, organization, and simplicity. Every young person will certainly recognize the value of this gift once they make this an emphasis. We will talk about several areas in the life of a teenager where the discipline of administration could be a great influence.

For now, however, let's look first at one of the great examples of this gift in arguably the greatest miracle of Jesus in the New Testament.

COMPANIES OF FIFTY

In Matthew 14:13–21, Mark 6:30–44, Luke 9:10–17, and John 6:1–15, Jesus was teaching a multitude of people who had gathered to listen to Him for hours. His words were food for their starving *souls*, but their *stomachs* were rumbling. Jesus used an interesting choice of words by telling the disciples to have everyone *"sit down in groups of about fifty each"* (Luke 9:14). Jesus was about to simplify one of the most dynamic miracles in the Bible.

It may have taken an hour or so, but more than five thousand people were organized on that hillside in small groups and then fed with the lunch of a young boy. (See John 6:9.) We can look into all of the ways it might have happened. But one thing is for sure: Jesus knew it was going to take structure and the gift of administration for this to take place. Everyone had more than enough to eat because after the five loaves of bread and two fish were broken and passed around, there were twelve baskets of food left over!

I HAVE LEARNED THAT SOMETIMES GOD ONLY NEEDS A SIMPLE PLAN TO DO HIS MOST DIFFICULT WORK. WE MUST EITHER BE THAT PLAN OR COME UP WITH ONE.

It was the simple planning that allowed for the miracle. As young people, we must develop the gift of administration and organization and see how it sets us up for God to do something significant in our lives. Young leaders must consider the kind of structures and systems it takes to see life success. Having worked in the church and now in education, I have seen that there are many small principles missing in teenagers' lives that could bring about big changes.

One book that has impacted me in this area is Jim Collins' bestseller, *Good to Great*.[5] The pages of this book are filled with concepts of organizational excellence that could be applied to youth in our culture today. Let me give you one of those principles that could take your discipline to the next level.

One of the lessons that Collins covers is the importance of both the character and the business traits that can transform a person and ultimately a company. Similarly, one of the things I have seen in ministry over the years is the close connection between character and administration. The heart and the hand are implicit in both organizational and ministry settings.

David wrote most of the Psalms. But his writer, Asaph, wrote about twelve to fifteen of them. In Psalm 78, reviewing David's leadership over Israel, Asaph tells us that King David guided Israel *"with integrity of heart"* and *"skillful hands"* (Psalm 78:72 NIV). Two things. Both the *heart* and the *hand* had everything to do with how he led. God blessed him because he was righteous and also talented.

Here's a list of the different kinds of disciplines that make up our *spiritual* leadership:

- The spiritual disciplines in this book (prayer, Bible reading, fasting, praying in the Spirit, etc.)
- Giving
- Encouragement
- Rest
- Worship
- Service

Here's a list of the different kinds of disciplines that make up our *natural* leadership:

- Administration and organization
- Vision casting
- Preaching, teaching, or communications and correspondence

---

5. Jim Collins, *Good to Great: Why Some Companies Make the Leap and Others Don't* (New York: HarperCollins, 2001).

- Creativity, research, and development

- Relationships and interpersonal skills

- Programming and systems

- Total wellness (physical, spiritual, intellectual, emotional, and the balance of one's intelligence quotient and emotional quotient, IQ vs. EQ)

It is much easier to understand these kind of spiritual and natural traits when we see them in a list. Now, let's break down what Psalm 78 says about these.

ONE OF THE THINGS I HAVE SEEN IN MINISTRY OVER THE YEARS IS THE CLOSE CONNECTION BETWEEN CHARACTER AND ADMINISTRATION. THE HEART AND THE HAND ARE ELEMENTARY IN HEALTHY MINISTRY.

THE HEART; INTEGRITY

The discipline of the heart is the first order of leadership, administration, and simplicity. This assures that every task we are about to undertake will be guarded by integrity and purpose. The heart is the spiritual discipline of placing all of our affairs in order. Beginning with the spiritual state of a person, organization can assist in the discipline of simplicity!

I remember the conviction and guilt that would overtake me when I did something wrong as a teenager. It was brutal. I'm sure it was because I was raised with a strong moral ethic...and got into trouble a lot. But it was that conviction and guilt that kept me from going too far down the path of destruction and countered all of the temptations coming at me.

At the core of every good leader is the *why*, the moral reasoning behind what we do. This is what is meant in Psalm 78 when Asaph reviews David's leadership and says he led with a pure heart. David loved the Lord and treated his people well. The heart is how we keep the reason for our work in mind with every task before us. An important spiritual discipline of every young person is to know why we are doing what we do.

If we can solve the *why* in our life, we can do every task as unto Christ. If we look at it this way, administration becomes worship. Organizing our life becomes praise to God. Living in simplicity allows us to focus on God and not stuff. The discipline of the spiritual integrity of our heart becomes the *why* behind all of the decisions in our life.

THE HANDS; SKILL SETS

Another great discipline for teenagers is the natural gifts of their hands, taking care of the giftings that each of us have. I love that Asaph said King David *"guided them by the skillfulness of his hands"* (Psalm 78:72 NKJV).

The discipline of the hands is the natural work of leadership. Skillfulness, grit, hard work, and the discipline of our natural abilities. This assures that every task we are about to undertake will be guarded by excellence and capability. The skillfulness of the hands is the natural discipline of a teenager.

At the core of every good leader is not only the *why* but also the *how*, the manual reasoning behind what we do. Psalm 78 tells us about the important natural work of David. He was a great shepherd capable of leading and taking care of hundreds of sheep. He kept them well fed by leading them to pastures and also kept them safe from harm. David was a skilled warrior as well, commanding armies and emerging victorious in many battles.

Every young leader must develop both their heart *principles* and their hand *practices*. It is when young leaders work with the principles of the heart and the practices of the hands that we see God's blessings on our lives. When a young person or an organization holds tightly to both of these, we see personal and organizational success.

WHEN YOUNG LEADERS WORK WITH THE PRINCIPLES OF THE HEART AND THE PRACTICES OF THE HANDS, WE WILL SEE GOD'S BLESSINGS ON OUR LIVES.

When it comes to spiritual leadership, the right conditions are set by giving God something to work with. Take the time to organize and think through administration of your personal life as a teenager. You will see the multiple effects on your life of *seating people in groups of fifty*. Let's take a physiological look at this gift for a bit.

WHICH BRAIN ARE YOU?

Each of us was uniquely designed by God, with specific strengths and weaknesses. This really is a remarkable thought. Understanding our design can help us work on things that perhaps we were not born with. That is why administration is such a powerful gift to those of us who may not be talented with it. There really are no excuses for a teenager to be disorganized because God has given us gifts to help us in our weakness!

The distinctions between the left brain and the right brain are obvious. The left brain is analytical, handling reading, writing, and calculations. The right brain is more visual, creative, and intuitive.

THE LEFT BRAIN

Mathematicians, scientists, analysts, and strategists are all analytical. Managers, organizers, administrators, and other leaders need to use the left brain. Let's say you are in this camp. Here's where you are going to be successful in the coming years:

- Developing systems and programs
- Shaping spiritual formation through information and content
- Creating clarity and structure through your gift of administration
- Systematically producing disciples through your teaching and preaching
- Drawing supplemental leaders around you who function in the right brain so that your implementation abilities will have ideas to work with

For left-brain people, this chapter is a celebration, a joy, and easy work because they see the value of this spiritual discipline. A healthy person and team will have a university of gifts and talents around them, assuring personal and organizational success. We will not do an analysis of brain wellness and team dynamics here, but it's important to note that a left-brained person needs those who function in the right brain so that their systems will be relational and interesting.

THE RIGHT BRAIN

Those of you who operate in the right brain might be thinking that you are at a dead end and unable to function in organization, or that it really isn't needed. You may be a poet, an athlete, a musician, a counselor, and often a corporate executive. Imagination, creativity, inspiration, colors, and relational abilities will be the tools of your influence over a generation looking for icons who are exciting and relatable. The social media world calls these people *influencers*.

Here's what right brain teenagers will do to be successful in the coming years:

- Creating systems and programs (as opposed to developing systems)
- Shaping spiritual formation through inspiration (as opposed to information)
- Creating momentum personally with their teams through their gift of aspiration
- Intentionally producing passion and health through teaching and preaching
- Drawing on supplemental leaders who function in the left brain so that their ideas can be implemented

Can you see the distinctions between the two brains?

My challenge to each of us is that we see, as Paul did in 1 Corinthians 12, that it takes all kinds of people to reach all kinds of people. As teenagers, take inventory of the type of person God has created you to be. That will assure your strategic influence in the youth culture. Our design is how God uses us to change the world.

Let's look at how the gift of administration and organization can be used in the life of a teenager.

ADMINISTRATION IN A TEENAGER'S LIFE

I love the emphasis of the apostle Paul in his letter to the people of Corinth. He was talking about doing everything with excellence, which is something every teenager should consider early in their lives. When we start building our lives with excellence as adolescents, we assure that our future will be built on a strong foundation. I'm sure you have heard the Scripture, *"So, whether you eat or drink, or whatever you do, do all to the glory of God"* (1 Corinthians 10:31).

IF YOUNG PEOPLE WERE TO APPLY EACH OF THE DISCIPLINES OF THIS BOOK TO THEIR LIVES, THEY WOULD BE WELL ON THEIR WAY TO BECOMING ALL THAT GOD DESIRES THEM TO BE.

Sometimes there is very little that sets one person apart from another when it comes to success. It could be something as small as the discipline of administration, organization, and simplicity. These are areas of a young person's life where patterns of discipline could yield great results.

Here are five areas where every teenager must use this discipline of administration:

BEDROOMS

Here's an area we don't often think would be a part of organizational leadership! In order for young people to change the world, they must be willing to make their bed. I'm sure that is listed somewhere in the Scriptures, but I haven't been able to find it yet.

What is accomplished by making your bed and keeping your room clean? Several things:

- *First*, if you do not get anything completed the rest of the day, you have done one thing for sure. You have made your bed.

- *Second*, by accomplishing this small task, you have created a win. And wins help us to be more positive about the other things we need to do that are coming up in our day.

- *Third*, if someone were to come over to your home by surprise, they will be impressed with your discipline...and not see your dirty sheets.

- *Fourth*, making your bed and cleaning your room helps you to organize all of the other things in your world, including your mind.

- *Fifth*, there is something beneficial about the atmosphere of a clean room. When dishes are taken out from under the bed, the garbage is emptied, and everything is in its place, there is peace and order in case you need to find something.

BACKPACKS

A simple organizational task, but this will help you to know where things are in each pocket of your backpack and get to those items quickly. I have often been saved from the discomfort of being rushed for an Uber, the metro, or a flight because I know exactly where everything is in my backpack. Phone chargers and cords, pens, keys, iPad, wallet, and snacks all have their place and are easily accessible. Taking care of the little things makes our life easier.

It may seem like a small thing, but bedrooms and backpacks are a great measurement of the kind of discipline that exists in a teenager's life.

SCHEDULES

Use your mobile phone to organize your mobile life! Placing your tasks and activities in a calendar can prevent you from going crazy because you are forgetting things. Some of the things you can include in your calendar would be your family schedule, school activities, athletic practices and games, church events, and your scheduled devotional time. Notifications can be set that will help you to be prepared and on time. When we use the discipline of administration in these smaller tasks such as calendars, we find that we're faced with fewer problems.

HOMEWORK

Maybe the most difficult discipline is to organize your school work, but it's certainly key to your present and future success. With so much riding on a teenager's years of education, organizing homework is a life-changing discipline. A teenager learns so many things in the course of education, including study habits, work ethic, time and task management, working with other students in a group, and the importance of grades and academic success.

One of the most critical reasons to organize your school calendar is to increase your scholarship possibilities. With the competitive nature of colleges and scholarships, the best grades are in line for the most money. Set your deadlines, due dates, and research times in your calendar and watch your grades soar.

CARS

If you drive, let's face it, your car could help you with securing a dating relationship with the person you have been watching. That wouldn't be the most important reason to organize your car, but it is an honorable mention.

In all seriousness, a clean car can help you avoid accidents. Don't believe me? Ever try driving with a dirty windshield? You also need clean windows on the inside to decrease glare, a phone charger that doesn't get in your way, and no empty water bottles that get stuck under the brake pedal! Proper maintenance and care of your car will also help it to last longer. Oh, and if you happen to get pulled over by one of our finest because you have been speeding, you will know the exact location of your driver's license and car insurance information!

FINALLY

The administrative disciplines and organization that go into these areas form a solid foundation to build the rest of your life upon. Our lives are made up of a lot of small but important choices that we make every single day—a project in school, an assignment at work, or even how serious you take making your bed as a spiritual discipline.

Again, I know that this is not sexy or popular to talk about when it comes to spiritual disciplines. But the Scriptures are clear that, *"Whatever you do, in word or deed, do everything in the name of the Lord Jesus, giving thanks to God the Father through him"* (Colossians 3:17). When teenagers start building their lives early as adolescents by doing things with excellence, for the right reason, they are assured their future as adults will be built on a strong foundation.

Look at this text again:

> *So, whether you eat or drink, or whatever you do, do all to the glory of God.*
> (1 Corinthians 10:31)

WHEN TEENAGERS DO THINGS WITH EXCELLENCE FOR THE RIGHT REASON, THEY ARE ASSURED THEIR FUTURE WILL BE BUILT ON A STRONG FOUNDATION.

When teenagers discipline their lives, it creates godly motives, and every task becomes worship to Christ. Whether that is a teenager cleaning their bedroom or organizing their backpack, everything else in their life becomes more successful. If young people were to apply each of the disciplines of this book to their lives, they would be well on their way to becoming all that God desires them to be.

SMALL GROUP APPLICATION

Quentin Winder, Youth Pastor • Lakeview Church, Indianapolis, IN

OVERVIEW

We should honor God with the time He has given us. Good time management enables us to live in a way that grows our righteousness, goodness, and what is pleasing to the Lord.

We live in a world that fights for our attention; busyness fills our schedules. I once heard it said, "God did not call you to kill you." If we want to be effective in ministry, we need to learn how to work out of rest.

So often, I would try to cram meetings in my schedule and answer phone calls and emails at home, just to show everyone how hard I was working. That only left me with burnout and fatigue, leaving my wife and kids with short answers and power naps. My priorities were not set in a way that allowed me to honor God and steward the time He has blessed me with.

Our world runs 24/7 but our lives on earth don't. We need to manage our time properly. What are your priorities? *"Seek first the kingdom of God"* (Matthew 6:33).

DISCUSSION GUIDE

BIBLICAL PERSPECTIVES

Time can be a friend or an enemy. How we manage our time can relieve a lot of stress, make a difference in our personal life, and ultimately improve the world around us. Read these verses together and talk about time management:

> *Remember the Sabbath day, to keep it holy. Six days you shall labor, and do all your work, but the seventh day is a Sabbath to the LORD your God. On it you shall not do any work.* (Exodus 20:8–10)

> *For everything there is a season, and a time for every matter under heaven: a time to be born, and a time to die; a time to plant, and a time to pluck up*

what is planted; a time to kill, and a time to heal; a time to break down, and a time to build up; a time to weep, and a time to laugh; a time to mourn, and a time to dance; a time to cast away stones, and a time to gather stones together; a time to embrace, and a time to refrain from embracing; a time to seek, and a time to lose; a time to keep, and a time to cast away; a time to tear, and a time to sew; a time to keep silence, and a time to speak; a time to love, and a time to hate; a time for war, and a time for peace.

(Ecclesiastes 3:1–8)

But seek first the kingdom of God and his righteousness, and all these things will be added to you. (Matthew 6:33)

I therefore, a prisoner for the Lord, urge you to walk in a manner worthy of the calling to which you have been called. (Ephesians 4:1)

PRACTICAL PERSPECTIVE

How do these verses support what Jeff said about discipline? How do these verses speak to priority?

The Bible shows us how important the use of our time here on earth really is. Balancing time with God, sports, school work, jobs, and other activities need to be prioritized with eternity in mind.

FINAL QUESTIONS

1. Do you have a set appointment to slow down and spend time with God? What about a Sabbath day of rest? Your spiritual health is important for your organizational health.

2. What do you spend most of your time doing that does not really accomplish anything? Is it removable?

3. Celebrate the small wins and assignments when they are finished. You will feel great about moving on to the next task.

4. What can you add or subtract from your day that will allow you to focus on more important things?

» *Prioritize.* Create a weekly list of high priorities (primary tasks) and low priorities (secondary tasks).

» *Attack.* Get rid of the distractions and attack the list by completing one task at a time, knowing you will be able to accomplish the low priorities faster.

» *Rest.* Make sure you block a day of rest when you don't do anything on the list.

Quentin Winder is the student ministry director at Lakeview Church in Indianapolis, Indiana. He has a great team of leaders who work with the youth and student ministry. Quentin has a passion for administration and organization. He studied at the Illinois School of Ministry.

SECTION THREE

THE
INWARD DISCIPLINES

We must worship Him with a humble, sincere love that comes from the depth and center of our souls. Only God can see this adoration, which we must repeat until it becomes part of our nature, as if God were one with our souls and our souls were one with God.

—Brother Lawrence

9

WORSHIP

(REVERENCE AND PRAISE)

The Practice of the Presence of God by Brother Lawrence, a seventeenth-century monk, was one of the first devotional books that I read when I was in college. It explains how to have a simple devotion to God in everything we do, practicing God's presence everywhere we go. It is a remarkable read and reminder that worship is a lifestyle, not a lyric.

First published over three hundred years ago, there have been many revisions of this classic little book with a singular message: how to practice the presence of God no matter who we are, where we are, or what we are doing.

The first conversation in the book relates a time when Brother Lawrence was only eighteen years old and experienced a profound impression of God's providence and power while looking at a barren tree in the wintertime. He realized that its leaves would soon appear, followed by blossoms and fruit, and this gave him a great love for God. He was learning to turn even the simplest of experiences into an opportunity to worship God.

Over my years in youth ministry, I have learned one important lesson when it comes to teenagers and worship: we do not have to teach young people to worship. They already know how to worship. They worship everything—materialism, icons, others, and even self. What we need to do is teach teenagers how to worship God.

WE DO NOT HAVE TO TEACH YOUNG PEOPLE TO WORSHIP. THEY WORSHIP EVERYTHING. WHAT WE NEED TO DO IS TEACH TEENAGERS HOW TO WORSHIP GOD.

To me, one of the most inspiring stories in the Bible is the depth of knowledge that young David had as a king in the making. Working in the fields all alone as a shepherd fashioned his musical and worship gifts in anonymity. Later, David's excellence at worship and playing music was evident while he served in the court for King Saul. If there is anything we have learned in the Scriptures about young David, it is that he was very gifted at worship and music.

THINK ABOUT THAT. DAVID, AS A TEENAGER, UNDERSTOOD THE PRESENCE OF GOD LIKE FEW OTHERS. HE WAS A SEEKER, A WORSHIPPER, A YOUNG MAN OF HIS PRESENCE—BEFORE HE WAS EVEN A KING!

Do you remember the story in 1 Samuel 16 about an evil spirit that would torment King Saul? Nothing could be done to soothe him and bring him peace. None of the seers or diviners who were called to court could stop the tormenting spirits that were howling in Saul's mind. His advisers suggested that he *"seek out a man who is skillful in playing the lyre, and when the harmful spirit from God is upon you, he will play it, and you will be well"* (1 Samuel 16:16). One of them suggested David, *"who is skillful in playing...and the LORD is with him"* (verse 18).

When David was summoned to the king's chamber to play on his harp, he did something nobody else could do. His worship made Saul well.

David knew God from a personal relationship with Him. That personal relationship was the fuel to David as a worshipper and a young man after God's own heart. (See 1 Samuel 13:14.)

THE IMPACT OF GOD'S CHARACTER ON WORSHIP

One of my favorite things to do in life is worship with teenagers. There is nothing like it.

When a teenager is abandoned to God completely, it will change their life. Worship becomes more than natural. It becomes supernatural, the direct result of the presence of God. Think about that. When a teenager learns the value of worship, they have an immediate sense of God's presence in their life daily!

In chapter four, we discussed the impact of God's character and nature on discipleship. We talked about how understanding God hooks a young person into wanting to actually know God.

Worship impacts a teenager in the same way. The knowledge of God is at the center of pure worship. In this chapter, we are focusing upon the musical nuance of the worship of God, mainly because we do not have the space to cover all expressions of worship, such as lifestyle, silence, contemplation, nature, poetry, spoken word, and kinesthetic.

I've heard many people say that young people today cannot be led in the worship of God. They say young people don't have the attention span to worship. They don't want to worship. They don't know how to worship. They are not spiritually interested enough to worship. Just wait until they grow up so they can understand it!

I don't believe any of these statements at all.

Why? Because they will binge a series on Netflix or another streaming service for hours and not move. They will play on a gaming system for hours and not get up to use the bathroom. They will sit watching a new movie for three hours and stare at the screen mesmerized.

Don't tell me that teenagers do not have the attention span to worship God!

It is not that young people don't understand worship. It is that they do not know God. Because if they knew God, they would worship Him. To be frank, teenagers probably have a better idea of worship than most people in our culture. This generation has the ability to worship sports, movies, and rock icons. They have even accomplished the art of worshipping self. Worship is what young people do in America.

IT IS NOT THAT YOUNG PEOPLE DON'T UNDERSTAND WORSHIP. IT IS THAT THEY DO NOT KNOW GOD. IF THEY KNEW GOD, THEY WOULD WORSHIP HIM.

Getting teenagers to worship isn't an issue. Getting teenagers to worship God is the issue. If we teach and model biblical worship in our personal lives and the corporate youth ministry setting, we will see this generation respond. Because teens have been raised in an idolatrous and materialistic worship of this world, it will take an intentional plan to place God back on the throne of their lives. To create a progressive biblical instruction and expectation of worship will work!

Just because we think teenagers are engaged with *world worship* doesn't mean they are fatally disengaged from the worship of God.

I want teenagers to see Colossians 1 and the nature and character of God. Let's not reduce God to sound bites and me-ology. We do not have to apologize to a generation that God is limited, lightweight, or cheap. I want the teenagers around me to see that God is big enough to be worshipped. That He is sovereign.

That God is above all, He is over all, and He is in all. That God is first, and there is no limit to His character and nature.

And it is just like God to give us reminders of His sovereignty. Look at nature and the world around us. It can be a constant reminder of how great God is. All of creation worships with us. And because God is a good Creator, we can see the presence of God in nature. Nature is part of how we remember the goodness of God and how we see our faith grow. To see God's creation is to stop and take a moment in the middle of the day to worship Him for His majesty and design.

Remember the illustration of the Grand Canyon at the beginning of this book. The only way you can actually get an understanding of the Grand Canyon is to visit it and stand on the rim of one of the great wonders of the world.

It is the same with our worship of God. Worship is standing on the edge of understanding God and brings us into His presence.

MUSIC AND THE TEEN CULTURE

It's difficult to get away from music in our world. Elevators, gyms, stores, commercials, and movies all have music in the background. Go to the mall, go to a game, or turn on the television, and you cannot escape music. Music has the power to influence the setting, build culture faster, and communicate more than most other mediums. And music cannot be separated from the teen culture.

Youth ministries are trying everything they can to reach students, including neutral site events, campus involvement, small groups, social media presence, and even multiple youth services throughout the week to give students different options to attend.

Here's a thought: because of the prevalence of music, videos, app-based listening tools, and the pervasiveness of music in our society, maybe one of the great ways to transform our youth ministries is through music—specifically our lifestyle of musical worship.

Worship goes against the grain of most youth leadership gurus and their pyramids or templates for growth, paradigms of leadership, or philosophies of ministry. However, worship is going to transform our youth culture.

MAYBE ONE OF THE GREAT WAYS TO TRANSFORM OUR YOUTH MINISTRIES IS THROUGH MUSIC— SPECIFICALLY OUR LIFESTYLE OF MUSICAL WORSHIP.

Teenagers love music. They are drawn to the emotion, the sound, the rhythm, the style, and *sometimes* even the words of music. What better way to assist an adolescent in discipleship and spiritual formation than through musical worship? Theology and worship are explosive!

As youth leaders, the clearer we can define the character and nature of God, the deeper the young people around us will see Him. The result will be a greater worship and presence of God in our youth ministry.

IMPROVING WORSHIP IN OUR YOUTH MINISTRIES

As we have said, the fine arts and musical passion of young people is a major character trait of this generation. This makes it even more important for youth ministry to have an intentional plan to increase the worship in the youth group and ultimately in the students' lives. Here are a few ways we can create a worship presence in youth ministry:

1. PROGRAM WORSHIP INTO THE YOUTH SETTING ON A REGULAR BASIS

Give it a priority. Whether you have a gifted worship team or have to use a video or audio playlist, show the students how important worship is by organizing it. Some of the really great moments in worship that I have had with teens were with video or audio playlists. Creating several of these for live worship settings incorporates sight and sound! If you don't have the musicians in your setting, find young adults, involve the adults in your church, or even ask another church to share their talents until you build the culture.

2. DEVELOP THE FINE ARTS GIFTS OF YOUNG PEOPLE IN YOUTH MINISTRY

Whether they play musical instruments, perform drama, sing, rap, read or recite poetry, or create art, there is no shortage of talent in the youth culture. Get students involved in the youth service, and they will own it and create a draw for other students to be involved. Open mic nights can create a great place for teens to display their gifts and for the worship of God to be creative and central.

3. DO NOT LIMIT WORSHIP TO MUSIC

There are many creative ways to inspire worship and place Christ at the center of our lives. This could include *stations* at the youth service where students read, write, speak, dream, or sit in silence. Encourage students to *worship live*, everywhere they are. Worship is more a state of mind and a relationship than merely a song.

4. MODEL SPIRITUALLY HEALTHY MUSIC TO OUR STUDENTS

Changing the music we listen to as youth leaders will increase our personal intimacy with God and our integrity before students. It will be difficult to convince students to worship God if we are listening to questionable music ourselves. Make the secular your sacred. Purify your Spotify!

5. TEACH STUDENTS TO WORSHIP IN PRIVATE SO PUBLIC WORSHIP ISN'T AWKWARD

My two greatest moments in worship were alone with God—not at a camp, convention, or youth service, not listening to a pop worship band, or even being with my friends. The greatest moments of our worship should not be in a corporate setting. This can be done by transforming our bedrooms, our vehicles, or our phones into worship tools. We must raise students who come to the youth group worshipping instead of coming to the youth group to worship!

6. CREATE NIGHTS OF WORSHIP WITH A VARIETY OF WORSHIP ARTS

Have an entire youth service set aside for worship, where worship is not simply an add-on. We have to remove ceilings and break fences around the students. Nights of emphasis can do this. Invite other groups and increase the community and the energy. This can bring a peer accountability to students when they see their friends in worship. If we want worship to become a part of the culture of the youth ministry, we must make worship a priority and give it more time in the youth service setting.

7. TEACH A THEOLOGY OF GOD AND THE WORSHIP OF GOD

If we are going to increase the theological knowledge and ultimately the worship of teenagers, we have to instruct students through biblical preaching and teaching. Correct teaching that encourages worship as a lifestyle will promote young people who *worship live* and not just at church. We cannot accept theological illiteracy. Teens can handle more than you think. I will deal with this a little later in the chapter.

DEVELOPING A PHILOSOPHY OF WORSHIP IN YOUTH MINISTRY

There is a fire burning in the hearts of American teens today. However, it may not be the fire of God. It could be the fire of sin that is raging like an inferno fed by idolatry, lust, materialism, fame, or even self. It is our responsibility as youth leaders to bring teenagers into God's presence. If we do that, they will transfer their passion to worship stuff or self into a passion to worship God.

THERE IS A FIRE BURNING IN THE HEART OF AMERICAN TEENS TODAY, BUT IT COULD BE SIN RAGING LIKE AN INFERNO FED BY IDOLATRY, LUST, MATERIALISM, FAME, OR EVEN SELF.

The 2005 book by George Barna entitled *Revolution*[6] includes an intriguing research finding that cannot be downplayed. They found that in 2000, 70 percent of people who experienced life transformation in Christ did so in the church. Only 5 percent of people experienced life transformation in Christ outside of the church. But the study and ensuing research indicated that by 2025, only 35 percent of people who experience life transformation will experience it in the church.

That is a remarkable finding—and disappointing. Not disappointing because people are being born again outside of the church in public, but because the church is not emphasizing the born-again experience in our messaging! That prediction, coupled with the finding that only 4 percent of Gen Z has a Christian worldview, must cause us to ask ourselves, "What is going on in youth ministry?" Gen Z has a larger percentage of atheists than any other generation in American history. We desperately need a presence-based focus in youth ministry, or we are going to lose Alpha Gen coming up next.

Worship and spiritual formation can be central within the philosophical approach of youth ministry. Look at it as a type and way of doing ministry. Here are two ways: *program-based* youth ministry and *presence-based* youth ministry.

I know these are generalizations, and both of these focuses are valid when done with intention and spirituality. As a matter of fact and practice, you can have both. However, that does not usually happen. In any case, there are some distinct differences in how these philosophies are played out in application on a week-to-week basis.

PROGRAM-BASED YOUTH MINISTRY

A *program-based youth ministry* is one in which the value is placed on organization and systems. The organizational win comes when the systems run well. A typical youth night may look like a pre-event with activities, opening music, announcements, a game, the short lesson, and small groups, in some order or another. There is little time for waiting and response to the systems. It is presentation-based.

---

6. George Barna, *Revolution* (Carol Stream, IL: Tyndale House Publishers, 2005).

In this approach, the ultimate goal is positive, but the outcomes are not always favorable:

- This is an attractional ministry model that defines success with numbers and attendance, not discipleship or spiritual formation

- The leadership are not trained well enough to build relationships with students and move beyond pulling off the evening agenda

- The music is mostly entertaining and nonparticipatory

- A short message or sermonette, if there is one, is entertaining and not very deep

- When small groups are done, too often, there is little discussion and conversation in the small group; it becomes a chat time recalling the day's events

- In most small groups, a leader takes over and ends up speaking 80 percent of the time

- Ultimately, there is no theological discipleship or spiritual formation

Again, this is a generalization, and I know there are some settings that can really pull off a spiritually-driven, program-based youth ministry. However, this is not the norm. In this setting, ultimately the evening has little experiential learning or expression and lacks theological practice of worship. Because for the ministry, the win is a presentation-based evening.

PRESENCE-BASED YOUTH MINISTRY

A *presence-based youth ministry* is one where the value is placed in the response to Christ in the organization and systems. It may be that each dynamic moves to a specific moment of response. There is ample time planned for waiting and response to the presence-based ministry programming.

In this approach, the ultimate goal is positive. And the outcomes generally are:

- A transactional ministry model that defines success as transformation, discipleship, and spiritual formation of the students

- The leaders build relationship with the students during the pre-event activities because the relational capital is key to the ministry

- The worship is participatory and responsive
- Messaging and the series are not just informational but also inspirational and leading to a response
- In this setting, the response could be individual or group-based but the goal is encountering and experiencing God
- In the small group based setting of this model, the student and leader are in a dialogue and the leader does not dominate the conversation; instead, each contributes about 50 percent

What we mean by building a presence-based youth ministry is that every program or system has an end goal of encountering God and His presence. The win is not kids having a blast at the pre-event, the game going smoothly, the twenty-minute sermonette being presented professionally, or splitting up into small groups at the end of the service. Rather, all of these things lead to a response to God and His presence at some point in the evening.

Programming done simply to be creative or fill a void is empty. The point or focus of programming should be the presence of God and students responding to this.

Here are four ways to build a presence-based youth ministry:

1. WE MUST EMBRACE THE SUPERNATURAL

We must promote signs, wonders, and miracles. The supernatural is a trait characteristic of the Millennial and the Gen Z set. If we are going to appeal to young people today, we must appeal to them at their felt-need level. Aside from other things, the supernatural is one of their felt needs. With no less than fifty-five supernatural movies and television shows out right now, it's obvious that entertainment merchants are capitalizing on this fascination.

HOW WILL OUR STUDENTS EVER LEARN TO WALK IN THE DEMONSTRATION OF THE SPIRIT'S POWER IF THEY NEVER SEE IT IN THE YOUTH SETTING?

Furthermore, Christianity is nothing if it is not supernatural. The foundation of our faith is supernatural. We must be believing for the demonstration of the Spirit in youth ministry. Youth leadership must teach students the importance of their faith and the gifts that God has given to them. Those gifts include faith, healing, and miracles. You could even include words of wisdom, words of knowledge, and prophetic words that bring revelation into the youth ministry.

Our students must be comfortable with the supernatural. Leadership must be committed to shaping an environment that allows for both a *definition* and a *demonstration* of the Spirit. That could be facilitated by youth leaders who are sensitive enough to know when to pause moments and when to press students to engage. If the youth group becomes a lab for the supernatural, our students' world will be the place their faith is lived out.

2. DO NOT FOCUS SOLELY ON SMALL GROUPS

To be honest, look at where that focus has gotten us today. Over the last twenty years, multiple organizations have driven the church to small groups. What has happened over that time is that 96 percent of Gen Z has a non-biblical world-view. I do not believe that is solely the fault of small groups. But if they are done poorly and leadership is not well trained, these groups merely become places to build relationships, not disciples.

Please understand, I am not against small groups. I've done small groups for thirty-eight years in youth ministry. I'm against small groups that do not lead students to God.

IF YOUTH ARE NOT LEARNING THE GIFTS OF THE
SPIRIT IN THE SMALL GROUP SETTING, THEN IT'S
REPLACING A VERY IMPORTANT ELEMENT OF
CHRISTIANITY—THE PRESENCE OF GOD.

Week after week, small groups take place, and there is never any room for students responding in worship or responding to the presence of God. Where are our students going to learn how to worship? Where will they learn the gifts of the Spirit? When is the last time you prayed for healing or for the supernatural in your small group?

Another thought here is that students are in small groups at school thirty-five hours a week. They're split up in classrooms and transition in and out of subjects all week long. Is that really what we want for them in youth group? Isn't there a point where they can only sit for so long, listening to a leader speaking 80 percent of the time while they vie for the remaining 20 percent?

My contention is poorly-run small groups that do not value God's presence are merely an add-on to our young people. They serve no spiritual purpose beyond letting them chat about life. Chatting about life has produced a 4 percent biblical worldview in Gen Z.

3. THE YOUTH LEADER NEEDS VISION TO BUILD A CULTURE OF WORSHIP

Too many youth leaders assume that they must not attempt the work it takes to grow a worship team in the youth ministry because they are not musical, or they do not have musicians, sound systems, lights, or adequate audio/visual equipment. Presence is not bound by musicians or equipment. We have to think beyond our limitations.

And yet, it is important to note that the reason many youth ministries do not have musicians is because there is no culture for worship. Musicians will follow vision. If you're a musician, you know what I'm talking about. There's an underground communication between artisans that goes through a region when musicians are valued. I've watched this in so many settings as the Holy Spirit has brought artisans to the church because of the emphasis on worship.

Here are some creative ways to assist the worship in youth ministry:

- Use a playlist that will help you set a flow to the whole evening
- That playlist could be beats for transitions and fill, or worship music for the set
- Using apps like Spotify and iTunes or YouTube will help tremendously in settings where there are not adequate teams of musicians—until you can develop them

- Reach out to people around you who are more musical

- Find the fine arts gifts and talents in your youth ministry, including art, spoken word, and drama

- The most important worship leader in every youth ministry is the youth pastor

4. PREACHING AND TEACHING ON A THEOLOGY OF GOD

Magnifying God in our teaching and preaching will cause teenagers to magnify God. We do not need to teach teenagers how to worship. We need to teach teenagers how to worship God. They already know how to worship; they worship themselves, others, their bae or their bestie, materialism, and icons. Getting teenagers to worship will be very easy if we introduce them to God. The only teenagers who are not worshiping God are teenagers who do not know Him.

Remember this in youth ministry: we are going to get what we celebrate. What do we spend most of our time thinking, teaching, and preaching about? Our youth ministries have a certain environment because of the culture we set. If God and His presence are valued, the students will respond if they are given the time.

We must teach students practical principles of worship. We cannot simply tell them to do something. We must teach them and show them how to worship. Spending a series on the different ways that we can worship will have a great impact on the youth culture and the involvement of students in worship. Singing, silence, dancing, lying prostrate, reading Scripture out loud, playing instruments, clapping, and shouting are just a few of the ways we can express our worship to God.

Students can handle theology. They are smarter than we think.

I'VE OFTEN HEARD YOUTH LEADERS SAY THAT THEY ARE NOT PREACHERS, AND PREACHING IS NOT A PRIORITY. DO NOT UNDERESTIMATE THE ROLE OF TEACHING AND PREACHING IN YOUTH MINISTRY.

I've often heard youth leaders say that they are not preachers, and preaching is not a priority. Do not underestimate the role of teaching and preaching in youth ministry. One of the best ways you can set culture and rally students in your youth ministry is the teaching and preaching of the Word in the corporate setting. Biblical preaching and teaching on worship is great discipleship for our teenagers and will yield a culture of worship in the youth setting.

FINALLY

If I fail to teach my students how to pray and how to worship, I've wasted their time in the youth group. I don't care if my students had a great time, if we provided elite programming, or if we were known for creative events. If my students had all of that but didn't learn how to pray or worship, I failed them.

In the tension between program-based and presence-based youth ministries, don't forget that we do not have to make a choice here. We can have both. They can complement each other quite well.

One of the challenges I have given to teenagers is to *purify their Spotify* so they wouldn't recognize themselves in thirty days. Worship is a great reset for any situation you might be in. In the middle of temptation, worship. In the middle of doubt, worship. In the middle of fear, worship. That kind of worship will change the atmosphere no matter where you are or what you're doing.

Young people already worship everything. We simply need to teach them how to worship God.

SMALL GROUP APPLICATION

Jarae Meriwether, Student Pastor • Lifepoint Church, Clarksville, TN

In this chapter, we discussed how prevalent music and specifically worship is to teenagers. As Jeff said, we do not have to teach young people to worship since they already worship everything. We simply need to teach young people how to worship God.

There are so many distractions to our worship of God. And it is just like God to give us reminders of His sovereignty. Nature and the world around us can be a constant reminder of how great God is. All of creation worships with us. And because God is a good Creator, we can see His presence in nature. Nature is part of how we remember the goodness of God and how we see our faith grow as a result of responding to God's design by worshipping.

Let me give you a text and a few questions that will help you become a better worshipper, even in the midst of difficulty and distraction to God's greatness.

PSALM 55:1-8

The book of Psalms can help us discover how to connect with God in every situation, especially in difficult times. You might think worship songs to God are always filled with joy, praise, and stories of victory, but the Psalms include worship songs that are filled with pain, grief, and even anger. Psalm 55 is one of many examples. It's a song in Scripture that expresses pain caused by the betrayal of a trusted friend.

INSTRUCTIONS

Read Psalm 55:1–8.

I don't know about you, but I can feel the anguish and distress in these verses. The author, King David, does not see a happy end in sight. He's in deep distress. He is shouting to God, "I'm not okay with injustice. I'm not okay with this grief. I'm not okay with what happened, God."

QUESTIONS

1. What are the difficult things you are going through right now? Talk about those.

2. Talk about a favorite worship moment or song that impacted you the most.

3. Think of a worship song that counters the hardship or difficulty you are going through and play it right now. Create several worship playlists on YouTube, Spotify, or iTunes

4. How can we use worship to deal with real-life emotions? You can worship in your bedroom, in the car, or on a walk. Worship has the power to change the setting and your attitude.

5. It's easy to worship God when our lives are great, but can we find a way to worship even when things look bleak? Think of at least two positive things that are going on in your life right now and thank God for those.

Jarae Meriwether is student pastor and a worship leader at Lifepoint Church in Clarksville, Tennessee. Lifepoint is one of the fastest-growing churches in America. His church places great emphasis upon the presence of God in youth ministry. Jarae hopes to challenge you with his thoughts and help you to lead a great small group around the topic of worship.

The purity both of the body and the soul rests on the
steadfastness of the will strengthened by God's grace.
—Saint Augustine

10

RESILIENCE

(FAITHFULNESS)

MY BROKEN PALACE

See, in America we all live in A Broken Palace. A place for beauty and beast. Of more and least. Where princes and princesses, kings and queens, where dragons and jesters all meet.

Where a frog is turned into a prince. Where princesses find slippers and princes to marry forever after. Well, that's how the story goes.

You know how the story goes. We write new scenes to re-introduce our old lives. We cover rusted gates with paint. We fix broken arms with Band-Aids. We beautify pigs with dresses. But you know, they are still rusted gates, broken arms, and ugly pigs.

My Broken Palace. Where Rapunzel wonders what it's really like outside the castle. Letting down her hair for a prince to rescue her from her despair. It may look like a castle but nobody sees the hassle. The struggle. The tussle.

It may look like a palace but nobody sees the malice. The loss. Or the dross. Cuz we all live behind the mote and the wall. Behind the shrubs and the façade of the castle. It's not what it seems. The marquee isn't saying who's really playin'. It's not for real. It's surreal.

My Broken Palace. Where we sweep our brokenness under the rug or put it in the closet or say we don't really have it. We ignore what we know is there for all to see.

That we hate each other. Get upset with our neighbor or a brother. We tell each other you're a bother. We tell our parents to shut up cuz we're fed up. Cuz we sweep our brokenness under the rug or keep it in the closet.

Since hardship and trial are part of Christianity and Scripture, why are we so upset about hardship and trial in Christians and culture?

We act like it shouldn't touch us, it shouldn't be us. Not in the U.S. And not in my palace.

But, this mansion, our bastion of hope and ultimate future, is where the pain becomes His platform. Where the mess becomes His message. Where the chaos is placed on His canvass. Where the tragedy becomes His triumph.

My Broken Palace. A palace where the King lives in His castle to rule. Where kings and queens are crowned and wed. Where princes and princesses are born

who live in broken palaces…and slay dragons.

There is a dichotomy to the palace we live in. In one concept, it's the *perfect* place. And the other, it's an *imperfect* palace. I like to call it *My Broken Palace*. It is beautiful, but broken. There are kings, queens, princes, princesses, dragons, and jesters all living together. It shouldn't be a shock to any of us that pain and promise, brokenness and blessing, all coexist—sometimes at the same time and in the same person's life.

All of us will have to face the reality of hardship, suffering, and loss at some point in our lives. Personally, I went through the death of my wife Jane in 2015. We had been dating and married for thirty-four years; we had three children and one grandchild together. Then all of a sudden, the beautiful book of my life included a chapter with the most pain and brokenness I had ever experienced.

But that is not the end of the story.

In God's sovereignty and timing, seven years later, I am married again, and God is writing another chapter for me. It is a chapter of promise and blessing as God brought Jessica and her three boys into my life. Now we have six children and six grandsons!

See, God redeems every moment in our life. He takes the *chaos* and places it on His *canvas* to display His grace to everyone who is watching. God doesn't waste hardship.

HARDSHIP IS SOMETIMES AN UNWELCOME VISITOR IN OUR LIVES. WE LIKE THE KINGS AND QUEENS, THE STEEPLES AND GARDENS, THE RIVER AND THE BEAUTIFUL STONE PALACE. BUT THE DRAGONS AND JESTERS? NOT SO MUCH.

The culture we live in embraces the concept of hardship. From birth through the educational process and even our vocations, life is hard work. I'm sure everyone recognizes the value of the soldier, the athlete, and the farmer in our culture. *Soldiers* recognize that the painful basic training will save their lives on the battlefield. *Athletes* understand that workouts will prepare them for a championship. *Farmers* know that preparing their soil and planting seeds will give them a harvest.

The cultural story in America is filled with references to hardship.

Commercialism, advertising slogans, and catchphrases scream, "No pain no gain," "Takes a licking and keeps on ticking," and similar messages. Look at the movie industry script writing that hails a beautiful thirty-minute ending after a ninety-minute ride of pain and loss.

And much like the cultural story, the biblical story is filled with hardship in many ways. Moses, Joseph, David, Esther, Daniel, the prophets, Mary, John the Baptist, Paul, the disciples, the apostles, and even the central figure of Christianity, Jesus, were all subjected to hardship. All of them experienced significant trial, sickness, and adversity.

We could read through the difficulties that each of these people went through and write a series about the loss, pain, and brokenness they experienced. However, we could also write a series on the gain, healing, and purpose that each had. Hardship seems to be the human condition since the beginning of time.

The faith of Christianity was born out of hardship.

Every teenager will have to navigate the difficulty of hardship at some point in their life if they are going to grow up to become disciples who are fully devoted followers of Christ. We cannot remove suffering from Christianity. That means that Christian teenagers must navigate hardship with the discipline of faithfulness and resilience. They must understand that the palace we live in is beautiful *and* broken, that our lives are complicated and sometimes unfair.

> **WE CANNOT REMOVE SUFFERING FROM CHRISTIANITY. THE PALACE WE LIVE IN IS BEAUTIFUL AND BROKEN. OUR LIVES ARE COMPLICATED AND SOMETIMES UNFAIR.**

I am reminded of the story of Job that guided me through the hardship, suffering, and loss in my palace. Let's take a look at the resilience and faithfulness of Job in the Old Testament book that bears his name.

THE STORY OF JOB

Job was an icon. He was extremely wealthy and known by all. His resources included land, buildings, pools, cattle, vineyards, and workers. He had a large family of ten children. Job was a man of integrity and high character in the land of Uz, in the Palestinian desert region.

With a life like that, you would think that Job had it easy. Living in a palace like Job with all of the stuff would certainly make life easy for him and his family. Right? Try again. It wasn't smooth sailing for Job. His story actually looks more like a nightmare than a dream because of hardship.

Job's story is one for the ages. He is one of the key figures in the Old Testament of the Bible and provides us with an interesting example of a life dedicated to God. For even though he was righteous and wealthy, hardship came down upon Job swiftly.

The story goes that Satan thought the only reason Job was so blessed was because God was protecting him. So Satan wanted to unleash a trial to test Job's faith. And God gave permission for Satan to bring hardship into Job's life. (See Job 1:10–12.)

With God's permission, Satan brought great loss of land, buildings, and property to Job. Satan brought death to the workers under Job's care. He brought natural disaster to his home, and all of Job's children were killed. Still, Job was *"blameless and upright,"* so Satan sought one final blow. He plagued Job with physical disease that covered his body with painful sores. The damage done, Satan leaves Job's story in chapter 2.

However, through all of the hardship that Satan brought into Job's life, Job never cursed God or sinned. What a story of resilience and faithfulness! He persevered in his faith to such a degree that to this day, we refer to "the patience of Job." In the end, Job's faithfulness in these trials rewarded him with a double portion of everything he had before the hardship, including the restoration of his family. Job's devotion is a testimony to the grace of God in our lives. God has the final word in Job's life—and He has the final word in your life too.

You cannot fully know God until you have suffered.

Many of us think that we are immune to difficulty because we are American or Christian. Contrary to popular opinion, you will find that culture and Scripture promote hardship as a way to maturity and strength. As Paul said:

> I want to know Christ—yes, to know the power of his resurrection and participation in his sufferings. (Philippians 3:10 NIV)

Our spiritual maturity and formation cannot be complete without hardship. If we seek the Lord in our trials, the loss and difficulty creates faithfulness and resilience in us.

THE SNOWFLAKE GENERATION

This is an infamous term for our generation. You know—soft, or fleeting, or lacking constancy. It means this generation has no constitution, needs *safe places* on the university campus, and fears the *language of trauma*. Did you know that 78 percent of us are unhappy with the way things are going in our country today? But why?

In an article published a few days before Thanksgiving in 2006, Craig R. Smith, now chairman emeritus of Swiss America Trading Corporation, wondered:

> What we are so unhappy about?
>
> Is it that we have electricity and running water 24 hours a day, 7 days a week? Is our unhappiness the result of having air conditioning in the summer and heating in the winter? Could it be that 95.4 percent of these unhappy folks have a job? Maybe it is the ability to walk into a grocery store at any time and see more food in moments than Darfur has seen in the last year?
>
> Maybe it is the ability to drive from the Pacific Ocean to the Atlantic Ocean without having to present identification papers as we move through each state? Or possibly the hundreds of clean and safe motels we would find along the way that can provide temporary shelter? I guess having thousands of restaurants with varying cuisine from around the world is just not good enough. Or could it be that when we wreck our car, emergency workers show up and provide services to help all involved. Whether you are rich or poor they treat your wounds and even, if necessary, send a helicopter to take you to the hospital.
>
> Perhaps you are one of the 70 percent of Americans who own a home, you may be upset with knowing that in the unfortunate case of having a fire, a group of trained firefighters will appear in moments and use top notch equipment to extinguish the flames thus saving you, your family and your belongings...This all in the backdrop of a

neighborhood free of bombs or militias raping and pillaging the residents. Neighborhoods where 90 percent of teenagers own cell phones and computers.[7]

Smith's comments were in relation to a 2006 *Newsweek* magazine article and poll that alleged about 67 percent of Americans were unhappy with the direction the country was headed. Here we are sixteen years later, and the negativity has only increased.

Not much has changed since then has it? This all made me think about what we have here in America. No, our country isn't perfect. But maybe we need a little perspective.

Smith went on to say:

Fact is, we are the largest group of ungrateful, spoiled brats the world has ever seen. No wonder the world loves the U.S. yet has a great disdain for its citizens. They see us for what we are. The most blessed people in the world who do nothing but complain about what we don't have and what we hate about the country instead of thanking the good Lord we live here.[8]

Maybe we have lost our gratitude and willingness to focus upon the beauty around us. Maybe our perspective needs to change.

What a description of *snowflakes*.

UPSIDE DOWN

I have a friend named Eric Samuel Timm who is an artist and painter. As a communicator, he has a unique gift of using art and painting to illustrate his messages.

One of the ways he communicates with his art is very interesting. As he is painting, you can barely recognize what he is trying to accomplish with his brush strokes. As a matter of fact, I remember watching him for the first time and thinking, "This guy is not very good. I could do that." The colors and lines

7. Craig R. Smith, "Made in the USA: Spoiled brats," *World Net Daily*, November 20, 2006, www.wnd.com/2006/11/38956.
8.. Ibid.

seemed confusing, and I couldn't make out what he was painting. I'm sure that everywhere he goes, people have the same response that I did, watching this distinguished and professional artist and wondering what is taking place on the canvas.

But as Eric's presentation progressed, I began to notice something in his work. And as he came to the end of his communication art, he did something very peculiar. He simply took the canvas and turned it right-side up to reveal the masterpiece. What made no sense to our eyes was now very clearly a skillful work of art. For ten or fifteen minutes, we had been observing Eric painting upside down. Once the canvas was turned right-side up, everything was clear. As great an artist as Eric is, it is the process of his illustration that becomes the asset. You have to wait until the end. And see from the artist's point of view.

SOMETIMES WE CANNOT MAKE SENSE OF WHAT GOD IS DOING. WE THINK, HOW COULD HE DO THIS TO ME? BUT GOD IS THE MASTER PAINTER, AND HE'S NOT DONE YET.

Apply this illustration to your own life. Sometimes we cannot make sense of what God is doing. We're thinking, *How could He do this to me? How come there is so much pain and suffering in the world? I thought that God was all-powerful?* What we need to realize is that God is the master painter. But He's not done yet. And when He is finished, He will turn everything right-side up so we can actually see what He has been doing the whole time.

The story of Job seems like an upside-down story. It's not right. Here is a man who was noble and righteous, a friend of God. And yet, the rest of the story seems upside down and *unfair*. But you cannot simply look at the beginning of the story. You have to read to the end of it, where God restores everything back to Job and shows us that He has a purpose for everything in our lives. And everything looks right-side up again!

There is more to the palace story than what we see. If we see our lives as a portrait, God is painting, and He is not done with the picture. When an artist begins to work, we might look at the portrait or the painting and think, *That's terrible. It's just lines and half-thoughts on a canvas.* But just like an artist's unfinished work, if things don't look right, God is not done.

The importance of going to the end cannot be overstated. Be careful not to get caught in the moment and miss the opportunity of a lifetime as you go through difficulty. Because someday, you will talk with someone who actually lived through crisis.

AT THE END OF THE BOOK OF JOB, WE SEE
HOW GOD USED JOB'S PROBLEMS FOR HIS PURPOSES.
ALL OF A SUDDEN, IF WE ARE FAITHFUL AND
PERSISTENT DURING HARDSHIP, OUR MESS IS
TURNED INTO HIS MESSAGE.

CONVERSATIONS IN HEAVEN

Can you imagine, at the end of your life, experiencing the mercy that allows us to enter heaven, having the opportunity to speak with the saints of the Scriptures and all of the Christians who have gone before us? What would those conversations be like?

In our presence for eternity will be the martyrs who built the church before us. The Christians who were tortured during the crusades. The apostles and disciples who walked with Christ and wrote the Scriptures we have today. The prophets from the centuries before Christ whose words are chronicled in the Old Testament. And the angels who have visited humanity since the beginning of time.

However, of great importance and interest to me will be my conversations with Job and the apostle Paul.

Allow me to stretch your imagination for a minute. One afternoon in heaven, you walk into the cafeteria and notice an empty seat over at Job and Paul's table. It's your chance to speak with two of the most iconic figures in the Bible, two of the central figures of Christianity.

As you approach the table with your tray, Job motions with his hand for you to be seated. Nervously you sit and are at a loss for words because of who you are seated with. And Paul simply says to you, "Hi, I'm Paul. What's your story, young man?"

Now, I'm not sure how they will speak in heaven or what language will be used, so stay with me. And think about this. What will be your response? Remember, you're sitting with Job and Paul. I think most of us will respond with something like this:

> Well, guys, see, I uh, I'm from America. The United States. And it was rough. I don't know about you guys, but, I mean, my school was tough on me. I went to See You at the Pole one year, and they mocked me all day long in class and at lunch. I had to stop bringing my Bible and wearing my church merchandise because they were so rude and condescending. Calling me names and stuff. And there were times when I thought, "God, where are You?" You know what I mean?

As Paul and Job turn and look at each other with blank stares on their faces, and then pick up their trays and walk away, do you realize what you've just said? To Paul and Job.

Let me remind you of their suffering. Of their hardship, loss, pain, and disappointment in life. In peril from family and friends, dangers at sea, sickness to their bodies, beatings from a mob, and imprisoned for the gospel. Let me remind you that they each were within hours of their life. And they lost their integrity before all of their family and friends for the sake of God. That both Paul and Job lost everything.

And you want to talk about friends who mocked you for going to See You at the Pole, or coworkers who isolated you in the office, or peers who were rude because you prayed for your meal at lunch, or strangers who laughed at you because you are Christian?

Listen, I'm not trying to minimize your problems. I'm trying to maximize your God.

WHEN GOD PLAYS CHESS

At the forefront of the discipline of faithfulness is trust in the designer of your life.

God and His ways are like a chess match, while our ways are like playing checkers. He is always working from a different perspective, a more strategic perspective, and a more thoughtful angle. Because He loves us.

Chess requires much more forethought and planning than checkers. There are so many moving pieces and options on the board when you play chess, so it's more calculating than checkers.

You can tell by your response to discipline what kind of person you are. Are you a fight or flight person? Have you been trained to contend or complain? Are you more willing to accept a challenge or reject it? Is it easier for you to play the game or deflect the blame?

WE HAVE TO TRAIN OUR MIND BEFORE THE HARDSHIP COMES SO WE CAN USE THE TRIAL FOR A TRIUMPH. BY TRAINING OUR MIND, WE CAN BELIEVE THAT OUR MESS IS HIS MESSAGE.

We have to train our mind before the hardship comes. By doing that, we will use the trial for a triumph. We will put our chaos on His canvas. By training our mind, we can believe that our mess is His message. Without a strong mind, it is too easy to get pouty in the problems. Don't lose heart in the hardship. And don't be selfish in the suffering. Learn to unlearn old ways that are not helping you respond correctly to hardship.

One song about hardship that has endured for more than fifty years is the Beatles' ballad "Hey Jude." This song evolved from "Hey Jules," a song Paul McCartney wrote in 1968 to comfort John Lennon's son Julian during his parents' separation.

> Hey Jude, don't make it bad.
> Take a sad song and make it better.
> Remember to let her into your heart,
> Then you can start to make it better.[9]

John Lennon once said, "You're born in pain. Pain is what we are in most of the time, and I think that the bigger the pain, the more God you look for."

The bigger the pain, the more God you look for. The bigger the pain, the more God you look for. That's not a typo. I wanted you to read that a few times. Think of it this way: the more we let God in, the better we will feel.

The Beatles' words are simple yet true. In our hardship, if we place anything before God, we frustrate ourselves with *replacement help*, ultimately losing the perspective and the possibility of what hardship and suffering are able to bring into our life. We cannot find relief in trying to run from pain because it will always be there.

Pain is faster than we can run, pain is louder than our silence, and pain will come into our mind even if we close our eyes. We find our relief and neutralize pain when we realize why we are going through it. We find our relief when we realize how long we must go through it.

Our idolatry can easily make us settle for less when we are going through difficulty. However, when we place God central in our life, we then allow Him to redeem hardship and suffering for His purpose.

The Beatles penned many famous songs that have almost become a prophetic prose for our culture today. With the rise of hardship and suffering in our world, the words from the apostle Paul, King Solomon, and the Beatles can all be sources of comfort.

The Beatles wrote:

---

9. The Beatles, "Hey Jude," on *Hey Jude/Revolution* (Apple, 1968).

When I find myself in times of trouble, Mother Mary comes to me
Speaking words of wisdom, let it be
And in my hour of darkness she is standing right in front of me
Speaking words of wisdom, let it be
Let it be, let it be, let it be, let it be
Whisper words of wisdom, let it be
And when the broken hearted people living in the world agree
There will be an answer, let it be.[10]

Thousands of years before the Beatles, Solomon wrote:

For everything there is a season, and a time for every matter under heaven…a time to kill, and a time to heal; a time to break down, and a time to build up; a time to weep, and a time to laugh; a time to mourn, and a time to dance; a time to cast away stones, and a time to gather stones together; a time to embrace, and a time to refrain from embracing; a time to seek, and a time to lose; a time to keep, and a time to cast away.

(Ecclesiastes 3:1, 3–6)

As Solomon says often in Proverbs, "*There is a way that seems right to a man, but its end is the way to death.*" (See, for example, Proverbs 14:12; 16:25.)

We have too many things that we have learned in America that must be unlearned. It may seem right, but it is wrong to think that we don't deserve hardship, or that we are cursed if it comes to us. That is spoiled Western thinking.

In the *university of suffering*, we are taught to think differently. Solomon was the wisest man to ever live, and his advice to us is simple. Our way of thinking is the wrong way. So we must listen to the Scriptures and to the rabbi.

FINALLY

The sufferings of this present time are not worth comparing with the glory that is to be revealed to us.   (Romans 8:18)

10.. The Beatles, "Let It Be," on *Let It Be* (Apple, 1970).

One of the great preachers of all time was Charles Spurgeon. Early in his ministry, he went through a very trying experience that caused him great pain. On October 19, 1856, while he was preaching to a crowd of over ten thousand people, someone shouted, "Fire!" Seven people were crushed to death as thousands fled the building in the ensuing panic. Two dozen people suffered serious injuries.

Spurgeon was filled with guilt. His message was on Proverbs 3:33, *"The curse of the LORD is on the house of the wicked"* (NKJV). Trying to calm the crowd, he continued to preach as people ran out the doors. Then he fainted.

Life became unbearable for Spurgeon. There were reports that two thousand people outside the building prevented the people inside from leaving. On top of that, the city and the media blamed the young preacher for what happened.

Although he would never fully recover from this disaster, Spurgeon's ministry continued. He later said, "I have gone to the very bottoms of the mountains, as some of you know, in a night that never can be erased from my memory...But, as far as my witness goes, I can say that the Lord is able to save unto the uttermost and in the last extremity, and he has been a graceful God to me."

How did Spurgeon recover?

It took several years, but the joy he exhibited after this trial was heaven-sent grace. Spurgeon's joy was based not only on his own ability to recover, but also on God's ability to restore him with forgiveness. The pressure of the press and the negative things that were being said about him actually stirred London to greater attendance at his meetings. More people were hearing the gospel and responding because of the tragedy.

Spurgeon had discovered the discipline of resilience.

SMALL GROUP APPLICATION

Heidi Rausch, Youth Minister • Minneapolis, MN

Resilience is a word that's not often used today. Once I share the definition, you may understand why. Resilience is toughness or the capacity to recover quickly from difficulties. It would seem this isn't a noun that could be used to describe this generation or the next. In a high anxiety, easily offended day and age, hard circumstances are doing a lot to take young people out. And some of them are walking away from their faith along the way.

Faith needs resilience.

I understand the statistics that show the greater pressures on young people today. From school stress to extracurricular stress to social stress, life is very different even from ten years ago. The rise in mental health issues is alarming.

Recently I had a conversation with a mom whose daughter had a breakdown in school. They were waiting for a bed to open up at any of the mental health institutes within the Twin Cities region because every bed was full! That's right—every bed within the Minneapolis–Saint Paul metro area was full of teenagers. We all know the stress that 2020 brought on most adults, but our young people felt it too.

Like in any relationship, our relationship with Christ takes work. There will be moments when you have questions, perhaps even moments when you disagree or are upset. Yes, you can be mad at God. But resilience says, "Regardless, I'm in this till the end."

True conversion in Christ is the kind that won't walk away no matter what. I'm coming out of one of my least favorite seasons, to put it nicely. I've reassured my family and even my youth students that I've been mad at God. I've been confused, depressed, and tired.

But I'll never walk away from Christ. I was forever changed as a teenager, and there's no going back.

So, how can we build resilience and faithfulness into our lives? Here are a few important steps:

- Surround yourself with other resilient followers of Christ

- See a counselor or talk to a pastor so that you can wrestle with the hard stuff in a healthy, open environment with a trained clinician

- Read the Word of God as much as you can because when you do, you realize there really is *"nothing new under the sun"* (Ecclesiastes 1:9)

- Remember, hardship is not personal; it's here because sin lives here

Resilience is hard work. It isn't stuffing everything under the rug and pretending it never happened. It isn't unfollowing or walking away. It's not sitting and focusing on your difficulty so much so that you bury yourself into depression over and over again. I certainly would feel no rush to recover if this world was all I thought there was. But the reality is there is more—there is the hope of an eternal kingdom!

Resilience is built through difficulty, no doubt, but it's built even more during the good times. Had I not spent time in prayer, fasted, read the Word, engaged in conversation, worshipped, and encountered the almighty God when it was all good, I'm not sure I would have had the strength to keep going when things felt tough.

Let's take this into the small group setting:

1. Tell a story of a time where you kept persevering even though you wanted to quit.

   » Resilience is the ability to maintain a positive spirit even in the face of adversity

   » On a scale of one to ten, rate how well you do at having resilience

   » What is faithfulness? Tell of a time when you were faithful.

2. Resilience is known to help with longevity.

   » Why would having resilience in our faith be important?

   » Why do you think this discipline can be hard to achieve?

3. Read John 16:33 together.

>> What stood out to you about this verse?

>> How does this apply to your life today?

>> What does this teach you about resilience?

4. How can we work to build the discipline of resilience this week?

- Offer ideas or suggestions after hearing them share their ideas:

    >> Shift your focus this week, from problems to praise

    >> Find someone mature in faith to open up to

    >> Speak from a place of victory – God has overcome the world!

Heidi Rausch, an eight-year youth ministry veteran, is a trusted voice in student discipleship. She is one of America's great young youth leaders who values her time with young people, small group discipleship, and spiritual formation in teenagers. Heidi has overcome multiple health issues and faithfully served teenagers through the hardship. She and her husband Chris and daughter Avanelle live in Minneapolis, Minnesota. Heidi received her bachelor's degree in youth ministry from North Central University.

In silence and in stillness, a devout soul profits and learns
the hidden things of the Scriptures.
—Thomas à Kempis

11

SILENCE

(SABBATH)

Maybe one of the most difficult tasks in this book will be to talk about the discipline of silence.

Let me say it as clearly as I can. We're like rechargeable batteries that sometimes run out of energy. Daily life takes its toll on our physical, emotional, relational, and spiritual health. Maybe restless sleep, deadlines at school, unhealthy eating, or broken relationships have you scrambling and overwhelmed. It's important to recognize the need for rest and the revitalization that comes from a Sabbath.

The Gen Z set—and now Alpha Gen set coming behind them—have been raised in the fast-paced social media world that has brought a global playing field into the palm of their hands. In addition, because one of the key characteristic traits of Gen Z is *production* and *publication*, any discussion of silence or rest seems irrelevant to them. In fact, young people may find silence and rest next to impossible. So how can we expect to have a successful conversation about these when their world is screaming, and teenagers feel the pressure of *production* and *publication*?

The false narrative is that America equates busyness with production. In fact, the quicker we slow teenagers down, the better. Having a night off once a month, no-phone Fridays, or even unplugged mornings can provide stress relief. We don't have to always be following, threading, thinking, posting, programming, on the way to another event, or looking for the next activity. The regeneration that takes place during a Sabbath is transformative to total health.

> **THE QUICKER WE SLOW TEENAGERS DOWN, THE BETTER. THE REGENERATION THAT TAKES PLACE DURING A SABBATH IS TRANSFORMATIVE TO TOTAL HEALTH.**

In what should be the greatest days in a teenager's life, the adolescent dream has turned into a nightmare. A thorough application of these spiritual practices will help turn the tsunami of busyness that is crashing on the shores of our nation's youth. One of the most impactful spiritual disciplines in the life of a teenager could be silence, rest, and a Sabbath, something that is not very popular today.

It's almost like we have turned busyness into a spiritual discipline. The idea is that the busier we are, the better we are. The American dream is tied into the oft-repeated phrase, "Time is money, and money is time." People boast that they are tired and burning it on both ends. They describe their life as if they are working overtime every week, as if they are trying to equate busyness with success.

I've been there. Feeling guilty that I have a day off. Feeling conviction if I sit down at the end of the day without checking my email or doing some correspondence. Feeling like a loser halfway through our vacation (if we take one) because everybody else is getting ahead of me while I rest.

Did you get that? Rest is spiritual. And in a society that promotes busyness, rest becomes less valuable.

WE MUST NOT SLIP INTO THINKING THAT BUSYNESS IS PRODUCTION. BUSYNESS HAS NOTHING TO DO WITH PRODUCTION. AND TO BE FRANK, WE NEED A NEW APPRECIATION FOR SILENCE—AND AN UNDERSTANDING THAT REST IS SPIRITUAL!

REST IS SPIRITUAL

We have seen a decrease in mental health and a feeling of purpose with a corresponding rise in depression and ultimately suicide in the Gen Z set. There are multiple factors contributing to this, including:

- The pervasive influence of social media comparisons
- The gaming, role-playing world
- The fantasy of artificial intelligence
- Online image and body shaming marketing
- The competitive nature of educational scholarships
- The spiritual vacuum of a generation

There are many other triggers, of course, but these prevailing issues take up center stage to destroy teenage mental health, self-esteem, and purpose.

The lack of rest is another major factor.

How do we counter the overwork and restlessness that causes depression in this generation?

Let's first start by defining depression. Depression can be seen as a severe dejection, sadness, and despondency. It creates isolation, confusion, and fear. It generally is considered long-term, but it can also come and go in various levels for a short period of time.

There are many troubling signs that develop from a lack of Sabbath, silence, and rest. Here are a few of them:

- Poor academic performance in school
- Withdrawal from family, friends, and activities
- Sadness and hopelessness
- Lack of enthusiasm, energy, or motivation
- Anger, rage, and aggression
- Overreaction to criticism
- Feelings of being unable to satisfy ideals
- Poor self-esteem, cutting, or bodily harm
- Indecision or lack of concentration and forgetfulness
- Changes in eating or sleeping or behavioral patterns
- Substance abuse
- Organ dysfunction
- Problems with the family, community, or authority
- Suicidal thoughts or actions

These should be the best days of a teenager's life. But young people don't have the necessary critical thinking skills to deal with restlessness and ultimately depression. A teen's perspective can be a powerful solution to any situation they may be in. However, they need to shift to the right perspective. We must help teens maximize God and minimize their problems.

Here's an easy illustration. If my hand represents my problem, and I place my hand on my face, I will not be able to see anything else. What I have to do is put that problem in perspective and move it away from my face so that I can see. Try that right now. Identify your hand as a problem in your life. Next, place your hand over your face. It is very difficult to see, isn't it? Now, move your hand a few inches away from your face and look what happens. You can see very well.

That is called perspective. It enables us to focus on solutions rather than problems.

THE SABBATH

The Sabbath has been lost in America. When is the last time you rested for a day? Can you remember when you last took a nap or spent an hour doing nothing? Stop equating busyness with spirituality. Christianity is more about grace and rest than it is about works.

GOD DIDN'T GIVE US A SUGGESTION; HE GAVE US A COMMAND THAT WE WOULD REST AND OBSERVE THE SABBATH.

The Sabbath is a commandment in Exodus chapter 20! God didn't give us a suggestion; He gave us a command that we would rest. Faith and rest will be a great cure for the stresses that can cause restlessness and depression.

There are so many Scriptures on Sabbath, silence, and rest in the Bible. Did you know that in the Old Testament, the people were required to rest their land from sowing crops every seven years? What a significant commitment to the health of their land.

Here are just a few powerful verses on Sabbath, silence, and rest:

> And on the seventh day God finished his work that he had done, and he rested on the seventh day from all his work that he had done. So God blessed the seventh day and made it holy, because on it God rested from all his work that he had done in creation. (Genesis 2:2–3)

> Remember the Sabbath day, to keep it holy. Six days you shall labor, and do all your work, but the seventh day is a Sabbath to the LORD your God. On it you shall not do any work. (Exodus 20:8–10)

Be angry, and do not sin; ponder in your own hearts on your beds, and be silent...In peace I will both lie down and sleep; for you alone, O LORD, make me dwell in safety. (Psalm 4:4, 8)

Come to me, all who labor and are heavy laden, and I will give you rest. (Matthew 11:28)

Then, because so many people were coming and going that they did not even have a chance to eat, he said to them, "Come with me by yourselves to a quiet place and get some rest." (Mark 6:31 NIV)

So then, there remains a Sabbath rest for the people of God, for whoever has entered God's rest has also rested from his works as God did from his. (Hebrews 4:9–10)

Sometimes the most spiritual thing we can do is rest.

SLEEP

Much of the body's healing work takes place while you sleep. Without the need to attend to all of the functions of daily life, your immune system and organs of detoxification, the liver and kidneys, can focus attention on cleansing and restoration. This is the time when your body does major housecleaning, taking care of wastes that have accumulated during the day and repairing cellular damage.

Cultivate the habit of going to bed early as a teenager. That will look different depending on the day, but before 10 p.m. is best. It is generally recommended that teenagers get eight or nine hours of sleep each night. Overriding this desire for sleep interferes with the natural rhythm of cleansing, brain function, and internal organ recreation.

Here are some practical ways to get the most out of your sleep:

- For the most restful and restorative sleep, make sure that your sleeping environment is not stale. Keep your room ventilated by running a fan to provide plenty of fresh air.

- Avoid eating for at least two hours before sleeping. This ensures that your body's energy can be used for healing and rejuvenation rather than digestion.

- If you do want to eat something before bed, a piece of fruit is a good choice. Fruit is cleansing and is quickly digested.

- Depending on the person, getting some physical exercise before bed is a great way to detox and wind down.

- A hot shower works for me every night.

- Organize your thoughts and activities in a journal for the following day before you go to bed. This will help you rest your mind.

- For some people, music is a great relaxation option.

- Try a noise cancellation app or machine if you need background noise to sleep well.

- Prayer and devotions in bed is a great way to fall asleep. (I'm only partially joking.)

The spiritual disciplines are a great way to end the day. Reading the Bible, worship, prayer, meditation, and journaling can help you free your mind and compartmentalize your thought processes.

TIME MANAGEMENT

We dealt with this in chapter eight on administration, but let's take a quick look at how time management can prepare teenagers to retreat from the many things that are making their lives so busy.

MANAGE YOUR TIME SO THAT YOU ARE ORGANIZED
ENOUGH TO COMPLETE THE MOST IMPORTANT TASKS
THAT WILL DEFINE YOUR LIFE AND MINISTRY.

If you are organized enough to complete the most important tasks in life, you will have a great advantage over everyone else. Your rest can actually help you to stay in front of the crazy schedule that is vying for your time and attention.

Every person should have *primary daily tasks* and *secondary weekly tasks* that define who they are and their life philosophy. Setting these important *daily* and *weekly* tasks in order will help you to organize your life. Although these will be different for everyone, this is what daily and weekly tasks or priorities will look like.

PRIMARY DAILY TASKS

Rest, nutrition, recreation, administration, family, hygiene, school, vocation, and spiritual formation should all be daily priorities. How much time you spend on these will be up to you. My wife has run every day for more than three years. Now, I'm not saying that has to be your new routine, but some type of recreation such as taking the stairs, walking, or stretching counts! The commitment you make to these kind of tasks will bring health, provision, and purpose to your life.

It helps me to schedule these daily tasks. This proves to me that they are priorities that should be done with discipline and intention.

SECONDARY WEEKLY TASKS

Friendships, homework, church involvement, extracurricular or athletic activities, part-time jobs, and social life will each need to be managed within a weekly schedule. These kind of tasks will not need to be done daily and can be a healthy part of our lives on a weekly basis. Again, the time management that goes into each is personal, but how we manage these tasks is critical to our success and sanity!

My life seems so much more resolute when these daily and weekly tasks are firm commitments.

A PLAY DEPRIVATION

One of the underrated areas of the Sabbath and rest is play or recreation. It might seem to be the opposite of rest and Sabbath, but play and recreation are powerful tools for bringing rejuvenation and wellness to your life.

PLAY AND RECREATION ARE POWERFUL TOOLS FOR BRINGING REJUVENATION AND WELLNESS TO YOUR LIFE.

God is interested in our total wellness—not just our spiritual and emotional wellness, but our physical wellness too. Maybe you are experiencing hardship or stress right now. Play and recreation are great ways to take care of yourself.

Years ago, I read an article and then watched the TED Talk of psychiatrist Stuart Brown on the topic "Play Is More Than Just Fun." I've always had a healthy commitment to the areas of recreation and wellness, but that talk challenged me to discipline my life specifically in the area of play. Out of that reading and the talk came commitments to nutrition, sleep, and exercise. But one area that intrigued me was play deprivation and my discipline to relax and play more. Going through the last few years of my life and all of the trials that my family and I experienced has increased the priorities for my personal wellness and play.

Now, I am not advocating a narcissistic lifestyle, nor do I believe that we must all become models of fitness that would take more time than we would give to our spiritual life or any other part of our lives. But I am speaking of balance and respect for our bodies so that we can perform at our best.

There are many reasons we must rest and take care of ourselves. This level of wellness can provide us with:

- Better daily performance
- Better health and quality of life
- A good reputation and respect from others and even ourselves
- Spiritual discipline
- Longevity of life

What does this look like in a practical sense? We can talk about nutrition, rest, and exercise. We can go to the gym, go for a walk, ride a bike, or get exercise in other various ways. Each of these are tremendous benefits to our physical health, and ultimately our spiritual, mental, and social well-being. But I want to speak about another wellness area.

PLAY

The benefits of play have more to do with wellness than we think. We have seen a lack of play growing in our culture here in the West. It could be that we are too busy or too lazy. It could be that we do not value play and so we see it as a childish effort.

Whatever the cause, a lack of play can lead to anger, loss of creativity, loss of confidence, health issues, little desire for exploration, and even social awkwardness. Thinking about these things should stir your interest in play activities, which can bring you greater mental and physical health.

A PLAY DEPRIVATION TEST

Ask yourself these important play questions:

- When is the last time you played with an object such as a ball, a squeeze toy, a jump rope, a stuffed animal, or some other plaything?

- How do you relieve tension or stress from your life?

- When is the last time you sweat from an activity?

- What is the last memory, conversation, or circumstance that caused you to laugh out of control?

Give an answer to the following questions by stating daily, weekly, or monthly:

- How often do you run?

- How often do you jump?

- How often do you laugh?

- How often do you make up a game in your mind?

The answers to these questions can be revealing. They are windows into our heart and mind.

SIDE EFFECTS TO A PLAY DEPRIVATION

What are the outcomes in our life from a lack of play? Maybe you have seen these kinds of things in your life lately. Could it be that you need a play date? I understand that my thinking is simplistic and quite idealistic. It will take a holistic approach to improve our total health. However, play will get you on the right path to deal with the following stressors in your life:

- No laughter

- Stress

- Anger

- Loss of creativity

- No confidence

- Health issues

- Loss of desire to explore

- Social awkwardness

FINALLY

These should be the best days of a teenager's life. After all, they live in America, certainly the most blessed and free country in the world. And yet, take a look around us. The youth of the twenty-first century have been born into terror, financial disaster, the break-up of the family, and a global health pandemic. They have been raised in a national setting of governmental division and an anything-goes entertainment industry. Teenagers and young adults have been immersed in the unrealistic comparison environment of social media, and they have seen an unprecedented sexual revolution crash on the shores of their life.

The pressure is real.

An October 2022 article by the American Psychological Association reported, "A majority of adults (62%) disagreed with the statement, 'Our children are going to inherit a better world than we did." Twenty-seven percent reported they are so stressed they cannot function.

And yet these should be the best days of a teenager's life.

The role of play can be a vital tool in the hands of a culture that experiences so much stress and is wildly driven. Play can be the answer to many of life's problems. So, whether you are experiencing stress or not at this time in your life, I have an assignment for today. Sleep. Take a nap. Dream. Play. Grab a toy. Don't step on the cracks on the sidewalk. Visit a playground and jump on the swing for a few minutes. Buy a kite, find a park, and fly it. And see if some of the tension in life subsides.

One final word from Jesus:

> *But to what shall I compare this generation? It is like children sitting in the marketplaces and calling to their playmates, "We played the flute for you, and you did not dance."*   (Matthew 11:16–17)

I don't want it to be said of me that I was too serious and missed an opportunity to slow down and enjoy life, to dance...or play. I believe what Jesus was saying is that we should become like children and respond to Him and the stresses in life the way they did.

They filled the streets with joy!

SMALL GROUP APPLICATION

Paul Sliwa, Youth and Young Adults Pastor • Church on the Rock, Wasilla, AK

In a world where things are instant and we are constantly on the move, where there do not seem to be enough hours in the day, we need to relearn the discipline of the Sabbath. One might think the idea of taking a break from work and having Sabbath time in life would be pretty easy, but our Western culture runs contrary to the concept of rest. Numerous studies have shown that today's teens are the most stressed-out generation ever, and as Jeff stated so well in this chapter, the lack of rest is a big part of that.

This is why we need to get back to the ancient practice of Sabbath that God established in the very beginning of creation. (See Genesis 2:1–3.) The Sabbath is a big deal to God and since even He took time for rest, we must realize how important it is for us to partake in Sabbath time.

Jesus also knew the significance of the Sabbath and practiced it often. Jesus was God incarnate, God in the flesh, and faced all the same temptations and challenges of life that we face. Even so, Jesus made time to get away from the busyness of life, be still, and rest. For Jesus, being still and taking time to rest was crucial for His ministry on earth; He taught us that God had given us Sabbath as a gift. (See Mark 2:27.)

The Sabbath brings us back to a place of dependency upon God and reminds us where we find our ultimate fulfillment and satisfaction in life.

DISCUSSION OUTLINE

GOD RESTED; READ EXODUS 20:8–11

- What stood out to you in these verses?

- Why do you think we are to remember and keep the Sabbath holy?

- If God took time to rest, what does that say about the importance of us taking time to rest?

LORD OF THE SABBATH; READ MARK 2:23–3:6

- What stood out to you in these verses?

- What did Jesus mean when He said, *"The Sabbath was made for man, not man for the Sabbath?"*

- How do we be disciplined in creating Sabbath time, but also not get too legalistic with it?

BE STILL; READ PSALM 46

- What stood out to you in these verses?

- How could rest and being still shape our view and relationship with God?

- What would it look like for you to find moments this week to be still and know that He is God?

MY YOKE IS EASY; READ MATTHEW 11:28–30

- What stood out to you in these verses?

- What does it mean when Jesus says His yoke is easy and His burden is light?

- Does following Jesus seem like a burden to you? Why or why not?

Paul Sliwa is the youth and young adults pastor at Church on the Rock in Wasilla, Alaska, the Next Gen pastor to several campuses in the Anchorage area. A youth leader to many of the cities in this region, Paul is having a lasting impact on youth ministry in Alaska.

God the Father we know. Jesus we know.
But, who is the Holy Spirit?
—Francis Chan

12

THE HOLY SPIRIT

(POWER AND PURITY)

The most important relationship you have on the earth right now is the one you have with the Holy Spirit. It's not your mom or dad, your brother or sister, your grandma or grandpa, your guardian, or your bae or bestie. Your most important relationship is with the Holy Spirit—because if that relationship is right, every other relationship will also be right.

Ultimately, a lack of biblical literacy has led to a lack of knowledge of the Holy Spirit. We cannot escape the theology of the Holy Spirit in the Bible. From Genesis to Revelation, the presence of the Holy Spirit is apparent, essential, and elementary. This makes biblical illiteracy the most common cause of a lack of knowledge about the Holy Spirit. You simply cannot miss it if you are reading the Scriptures.

It is certain that we need a greater understanding of God to fully comprehend His triune nature. Unfortunately, I fear that we have missed a complete understanding of God and made the Trinity a duality or a cosmic duo of sorts that includes God the Father and God the Son, Jesus. But we have removed the Holy Spirit from His place in the Trinity.

246 NEXT GEN *FAITH*

THE HYPOSTATIC UNION

That God is both divine and human, both Spirit and flesh, is a powerful truth that all of us need to understand. In the Scriptures, we find this concept of the *incarnation*—the human nature of Christ, of the Godhead—and the mystery of the Trinity. God the Father, God the Son, and God the Holy Spirit exist as One in the persons of the Trinity. Thus, the hypostatic union is the spiritual and the material presence of God in human history.

Understanding the Holy Spirit is similar to understanding God. Think about how we describe God. We have heard of His mercy, grace, love, patience, long-suffering, goodness, blessing, and faithfulness. But what about His justice, holiness, vengeance, anger, awesomeness, glory, heaviness, and power?

> *OUR VIEW OF GOD HAS BECOME CULTURAL AND NOT SCRIPTURAL. IF WE HAVE SUCH A LIMITED OR POPULAR VIEW OF GOD, THEN WE WILL ALSO HAVE A LIMITED VIEW OF THE HOLY SPIRIT.*

Do you see the discrepancy? Our view of God has become *cultural* and not *scriptural*. If we have such a *limited* or *popular* view of God, then we will also have a limited view of the Holy Spirit. To know God the Father and Jesus the Son is to know the Holy Spirit. And to know the Holy Spirit is to know the Father and the Son.

This is what Jesus talked about in John 14:7; when we have a relationship with the Holy Spirit, then we will know Jesus and the Father because the Spirit will take everything from the Father and the Son and disclose it to the world!

Let's take a quick look at a *theology* and a *history* of the Holy Spirit.

A THEOLOGY OF THE HOLY SPIRIT

One of the things I want you to understand in this chapter is that the Holy Spirit is a person. He is not an *it* or an idea. The Holy Spirit is a person. As the third person of the Trinity, here are the roles the Holy Spirit has in our lives:

- *Salvation.* He comes to inspire us to repentance. Acts 1:5 says, *"John baptized with water, but you will be baptized with the Holy Spirit not many days from now."* John 1:24–34 says there are two baptisms. John the Baptist's baptism was of water and repentance; Jesus's baptism was *"with the Holy Spirit"*—that is fire and power.

- *Truth.* With the rise in religious pluralism, the prevalence of postmodernism and paganism, and the lukewarmness in the church, the presence of the Holy Spirit is a crucial part of the movement of Christianity and the kingdom of God to walk in truth. (See John 14:16; 16:13.)

- *Conviction.* One of the key roles of the Holy Spirit is to bring conviction of sin and holiness, beginning in the church and then in culture. (See John 16:8–11.)

- *Power.* His main role is to give Christians power to be effective witnesses for Christ. (See Acts 1:8.) And a secondary work of the Spirit is acting upon us in a supernatural way for the work of the kingdom.

- *Gifts.* The Holy Spirit gives us gifts for the purpose of evangelism. (See 1 Corinthians 12:1–11.)

The gifts of the Holy Spirit are mentioned in Luke 12:11–12, Acts 1–2, Romans 12, and 1 Corinthians 12. They include the following key gifts:

- *Mission.* He has given us everything we need for our end-time mission and purpose.

- *Empowerment.* The Spirit empowers His people for works of service.

- *Wisdom.* Words from the Scriptures come from the Spirit in your daily life and as you study.

- *Knowledge.* Words of the Spirit come directly from discernment.

- *Faith.* The Spirit bestows an extra ability to believe in God's promises.

- *Healing.* The Spirit gives us the faith to heal and push through for people and encourage them for healing.

- *Effecting Miracles.* God intervenes when you act upon your faith by praying for people.

- *Prophecy.* Foretelling and warning from the Scriptures prepares people for the Spirit's leading.

- *Discernment*. Spiritual sensitivity leads to wisdom, action, and warning.

- *Tongues*. This gift includes private and public use of groanings that are too deep for words.

- *Interpretation of Tongues*. This gift involves the interpretation of the public use of tongues.

A HISTORY OF THE HOLY SPIRIT

Examining the role of the Holy Spirit in the Bible can help us see the complete theology of the Spirit as He was working in human history.

CREATION AND THE GENESIS OF HUMANKIND

The Holy Spirit was present at the beginning in Genesis and began His work by moving and hovering over the void that was before creation. (See Genesis 1:2.) Thus the Holy Spirit's work began in human history as the executive of creation. You might say that God the Father thought all of this, Jesus spoke it, and the Holy Spirit began to create it all.

FROM THE BEGINNING OF TIME, THE TRINITY EXISTED
AND OPERATED TOGETHER. WHAT MAKES US THINK
THE HOLY SPIRIT, WHO WAS IN THE BEGINNING,
WOULD NOT BE HERE WITH US IN THE END?

LAW AND THE WORDS OF GOD IN
THE TEN COMMANDMENTS

The Holy Spirit was also working in the age of the Law. Do you remember when Moses went up to the mountain to meet with God and receive the Ten Commandments? While Moses met with God, the Holy Spirit descended upon the mountain and as Moses came down from the mountain to address the people, *"the skin of his face shone"* (Exodus 34:30). The light was the Holy Spirit resting upon Moses after he received the Ten Commandments.

PROPHETS AND THE CALL TO REPENTANCE IN ISRAEL

The Holy Spirit can be seen very clearly in the age of the prophets. Multiple times, we see the presence of the Holy Spirit upon the prophets and their words—the Spirit coming upon Isaiah, the Spirit calling Jeremiah, the Spirit and fire over Israel as Ezekiel prophesied, and Joel prophesying that the Spirit would be poured out on all generations. (See Isaiah 61:1; Jeremiah 1; Ezekiel 20–21; Joel 2:28–29.) These are just a few of the many references to the Holy Spirit upon the prophets.

MESSIANIC OUTPOURING OF THE SPIRIT UPON CHRIST AT HIS BAPTISM

The Holy Spirit came upon Christ Himself. Now there is a thought. Even Jesus needed the Holy Spirit. This is a remarkable thought if you follow the Scriptures on this idea. Jesus's public ministry really didn't begin until the moment of His baptism by John and the Spirit's descent upon Him as He rose out of the water in front of a large crowd. It was then that Jesus began to do everything we read in the Gospels. Jesus even spent about four chapters of the New Testament (John 14–17, as well as other passages) talking about the importance and the necessity of the Holy Spirit. And if Jesus needed the Holy Spirit, then certainly we do too.

THE APOSTLES AND THE BUILDING OF THE CHURCH AFTER CHRIST'S ASCENSION

The Holy Spirit is properly introduced in Acts 1–2 as He came upon the disciples and the apostles after Jesus ascended. Jesus had been speaking to them about the need for the Holy Spirit for weeks. Now it begins with the outpouring of the Spirit on them in Jerusalem as the disciples and apostles build the church and take the message of Christ to the Mediterranean region.

Do you know that we are living in the same era as the apostles right now? It is the Holy Spirit who is the architect of the church era we are living in today.

And this is the dilemma.

If we do not have a relationship with the Holy Spirit, we will miss what God is doing in human history. We are living in the Holy Spirit's era right now! He was sent by Jesus to build the kingdom of God, and the Spirit is moving all over the world. But if we do not recognize His presence, then we will have no relationship with Him and what He is doing on the earth today. Ultimately, without a relationship with the Holy Spirit, we will have no effect upon this world.

IF WE DO NOT HAVE A RELATIONSHIP WITH THE HOLY SPIRIT, WE WILL MISS WHAT GOD IS DOING IN HUMAN HISTORY. IT IS THE HOLY SPIRIT'S ERA RIGHT NOW!

THE HOLY SPIRIT AND YOUNG PEOPLE

The Holy Spirit is active in human history. The Holy Spirit has used a young person in every generation to build the kingdom of God. *And you are next.* America is in desperate need of a revival brought by the Holy Spirit. Where evil rises, grace should also! The church must meet culture with a hope and healing for our nation with the Holy Spirit's presence and power. The Holy Spirit comes alive in every generation where there is such great need.

Look at the Holy Spirit in history:

- *He was working in creation.*

As we stated earlier, the Holy Spirit was in the beginning of time in creation, was also at work during the giving of the Law, and spoke to the prophets.

- *He was working in middle history as well as modern times.*

During the Dark Ages, when the church's voice was being hidden by crusades killing Christians, the Holy Spirit was filling the martyrs with power to witness as they were being slain publicly. And He was in the revivals of the last two or three centuries through the Great Awakenings, the South American healing revivals, the African crusades that drew millions of people, and even the supernatural growth of the underground church in China.

- *He is with us today in the twenty-first century.*

The Holy Spirit is working today in the age of the Spirit. The following are things that many believe will be marks of this next generation. We can see what the Holy Spirit is doing all across the world. Some people have given up on Christianity, but even in the midst of this present darkness in America, God is still alive and moving.

Look at some of the significant markers that many prophetic seers have been foretelling for the days to come. The theme that runs through these prophetic words is definitely the younger generation and their place in the coming Great Awakening:

- The twenty-first century will be one of harvest and hostility in Christianity.
- New media technology will help spread the gospel globally.
- All Christians will help the helpless and become taskers like Generation Z.
- A humanitarian wave will come from the church and will cover the earth.
- Young leaders will step into place in every segment of society when leadership shifts.
- Internal government affairs and failure will cause the gospel to spread.
- Heathen, Jewish, and Muslim leaders will declare their faith in Jesus Christ as Lord.
- Theology and the arts will blend to create a deeper expression of worship.
- The young people of the church worldwide will be more interconnected than ever.
- Public supernatural signs, wonders, and miracles will happen and draw people to Christ.

The Holy Spirit has used a young person in every generation.

Look at *Moses* being called to lead a million people as an adolescent, *Esther* saving a whole generation, *Rahab* putting her life on the line for her friends, *David* fearlessly taking on lions, bears, giants, and rulers, and young *King Josiah*, who led a nation at age eight and began to purge it of its idols at age sixteen.

WE CANNOT UNDERESTIMATE THE PLAN THAT GOD HAS TO REACH THIS PLANET. IT INVOLVES THIS GENERATION—AND THAT MEANS YOU, THE AMERICAN CHRISTIAN TEENAGER LED BY THE SPIRIT.

How about *Daniel*? The Spirit came upon Daniel as a sentinel to an entire nation as a young man, and he moved kings and leaders in the wake of the Spirit. *Mary*, the mother of Jesus, was a young virgin when the Spirit came upon her so that she gave birth to Jesus and raised Him in the Law and the Spirit. Even *Jesus* was not afraid to surrender His will as a child to be used in the mysterious plan of God. Finally, *Peter* and *Paul* were revolutionized by the Spirit, authored most of the New Testament, and built the church in the Mediterranean region.

In more recent history, *Augustine* helped rebuild the broken Roman Empire, the *monks* awakened the Dark Ages, *Martin Luther* and *John Wesley* began the Great Awakenings, and *Billy Graham* and *Reinhard Bonnke* led hundreds of thousands of people to Christ. Each of these Spirit-led leaders were called by God as children or teenagers and followed the call of God to transform their world.

The Scriptures and history are filled with the work of the Holy Spirit upon young culture shapers. Here are a few more:

George Whitefield began to preach in college and was one of the greatest preachers of the 1700s, often speaking to crowds in excess of 30,000 people with no amplification.

Jonathan Edwards was a young preacher in Northampton, Massachusetts, and he had a great influence on the youth there. He wrote:

In the latter part of December 1734, the Spirit of God began to set in extraordinarily and to work wonderfully among us. Very suddenly, one after another, five or six people were miraculously converted... [One young woman] told me that God had given her a new heart, truly broken and sanctified...Through my private conversations with many of the people, I have had abundant opportunity to know the effect this woman's story had on them. The news of it seemed to be almost like a flash of lightning on the hearts of young people all over the town and on many others. Those people among us who used to be furthest from seriousness, and who I most feared would make a mockery of her story, seemed to be awakened by it.[11]

There's no doubt that the Holy Spirit was using some of the youth in America like Jonathan Edwards to shape this nation and put an unforgettable and undeniable mark of Christianity on our country.

At age fifteen, *Billy Graham* attended a tent revival and was called to preach when a young evangelist named Mordecai Ham spoke in North Carolina in 1934.

Yale College had a significant awakening in 1796 when twenty-six Yale students founded an organization on campus called the Moral Society, which discouraged profanity, immorality, and drinking. By 1800, nearly one half of the college students were members, and this group is credited with laying the foundation for four revivals that occurred later on that campus in the first few decades of the nineteenth century.

Reiji "Ray" Hoshizaki was instrumental in sparking an awakening at Baylor University in Texas in 1945. God moved in a seemingly impossible or unlikely situation and used it for good. In the midst of World War II, the Lord raised up Hoshizaki, a young Japanese American believer, and used him to spark a revival at Baylor that saw hundreds come to Christ and be sent all over the world. What began with a handful of students sparked revival meetings that expanded beyond Baylor, extending through Texas and around the world.

---

11. Jonathan Edwards, *The Surprising Work of God* (New Kensington, PA: Whitaker House, 1997), 20–21.

Time magazine called the *Jesus Movement* in 1967 in central California the greatest spiritual moment in America's history. The awakening spread to the entire country in one decade—without social media. Politicians, educators, businessmen and women, entertainers, and athletes were all impacted by this move of God that lasted only about ten or twelve years. But the impact was undeniable.

A revival broke out at *Asbury College in Wilmore, Kentucky,* in 1970, and God was sovereignly moving in a variety of different ways all across America, but especially among the youth counterculture. The February 9, 1971, issue of *Look* magazine quoted one very optimistic minister as saying, "It's the greatest awakening in the history of the Church, and it's kids. Kids are leading it."

A group of about ten teenagers in Texas started See You at the Pole in 1990. The global teenage prayer meeting is held annually on school campuses the last Wednesday in September. The teens who started the event felt led to pray at several area schools during a weekend youth group retreat. Today, more than 7.1 million teenagers, including 4.5 million teens in America, gather around flag poles to pray and ask God for a spiritual awakening.

EVERY AWAKENING OF SIGNIFICANCE IN AMERICA WAS BEGUN BY YOUNG PEOPLE. IT MAY HAVE BEEN SUSTAINED BY ADULTS, BUT YOUNG PEOPLE PROVIDED THE SPARK.

What the Holy Spirit can do through young people is inspiring. History is clear that every awakening of significance in America was begun by young people. It may have been sustained by adults, but young people provided the spark. The Spirit of Jesus is no less powerful and real today.

But Western Jesus followers in the twenty-first century have yet to see an awakening of epic or viral or supernatural proportions as the Jesus Movement of the 1960s and Seventies. Whether that is due to materialism that causes a lack of dependence upon God, postmodernism that has given America a breadth of gods and religions to turn to, or the paralysis of the church, we haven't seen a significant revival in the lifetime of U.S. teenagers.

FINALLY

If there was ever a time in America's history that we needed an awakening, it is now. We are raising a generation that has never seen a revival or spiritual awakening. The Brownsville Outpouring twenty-five years ago was the last significant spiritual movement in America. And yet it did not really shake our nation or shift the culture like the Jesus Movement did.

Think about it. There hasn't been a spiritual awakening of significance since the Jesus Movement. Generation X was just born at the beginning of the Jesus Movement, and the Millennials were born at the end. Generation Z has never seen a spiritual awakening in their lifetimes.

Just like these moments in history, I believe we are on the edge of another awakening in our nation. It may not be close for various reasons, the foremost of which is our lack of repentance in America, but it is coming nonetheless. No doubt, it will certainly take repentance and brokenness like we have seen in every other awakening in history.

We have seen the Holy Spirit's work in every age of humanity. I believe He is about to do His greatest work for a world in the midst of its greatest need. I believe the Holy Spirit will revive the church, awaken a world in need of Christ, and draw them to the church.

We have a crisis in this generation: we are raising a generation that serves a God they do not know. It is my prayer that this book will help them to see the spiritual disciplines that will lead them to Christ through the powerful relationship of the Holy Spirit.

My prayer over this generation is that they will come to serve a God they know. My prayer is that young people today will model a special relationship with the Holy Spirit to the next generation, just like the saints of old throughout human history modeled to us.

SMALL GROUP APPLICATION

Whitney Tellez, Youth Minister • Scottsdale, AZ

Our first responsibility is to pray for the assistance of the Holy Spirit. We have tried so many things that have failed to jump-start this generation in the past. Education, entertainment, media, and even the church have had short life cycles and then seemingly fizzled.

There has been one consistent influence upon history: the work of the Holy Spirit and His gifts upon young people. Without these gifts, we lose the power Christ bestowed upon all believers. Throughout history, the Holy Spirit's influence has been evident in the lives of young people such as Moses, David, Esther, and Jesus, Peter, and Paul.

The examples we see in each of these people provide great illustrations of the power of the Holy Spirit to bring transformation and power into our lives. You and I need the same work. If these iconic leaders in the Bible needed the power of the Spirit upon them, then each of us definitely need it too.

After reading through the Scriptures from this chapter, discuss the following questions:

- What is the hypostatic union?
- When is the last time you saw a miracle or the work of God?
- How is the Holy Spirit a Helper to you?
- What is one thing you want God to do in your life this month?
- Which of the gifts of the Holy Spirit do you feel you need the most?
- How has praying in the Spirit changed your life?

Whitney Tellez has been in youth ministry for the last eight years and has a passion for the discipleship of this generation. She has led an extension college for young people to complete their degrees and be used in the kingdom of God. Whitney received her bachelor's degree in youth and family ministry from North Central University. She and her husband Darrison have two young daughters and pastor at Impact Church in Scottsdale, Arizona.

If the future of the church is in the hands of the
young people I see across this nation,
the future of the church is in great hands.
—Jeff Grenell

CONCLUSION:
THE FUTURE OF YOUTH
MINISTRY

Our greatest responsibility in the church is next gen ministry. Today's young people are tomorrow's leaders in both the church and society. We need youth leaders who are focused on greater theological development and committed to longevity in their work. This will require more thought and strategic planning within the church.

A youth leader should be one of God's sociologists. The principle is simple. Just like Issachar, one of the tribes of Israel, youth ministers should be people *"who understood the times and knew what* [they] *should do"* (1 Chronicles 12:32 NIV).

To understand the times is not easy. Knowing what to do is harder still. Looking at the current trends in youth culture and society, is there something that we can learn moving forward? Are there certain things happening now that will shape the future of our work? Looking into the future of youth ministry is exciting—and unpredictable.

There are many principles or ethics that should be part of the discipline and philosophy of youth ministry. Here are four:

- The *contextual ethic* and the importance of missiology in the world and the culture of teenagers
- The *diversity ethic* and the broad make-up of the Generation Z and Alpha Gen sets
- The *family ethic* and the need for rebuilding the integrity of the family structure
- The *sexuality ethic* and the critical need for identity and the sanctity of gender

However, I think we have proven in this work that the most important ethic for the future of youth ministry is the *theological ethic* and the need for spiritual formation and discipleship in youth ministry.

A QUICK HISTORY OF YOUTH MINISTRY

Perhaps looking at the history of youth ministry can give us a fuller perspective of its future.

Historically, every generation has had issues with youth. Whether due to jealousy, lack of understanding, or *ephebiphobia*, the fear of youth, younger generations have faced animosity from their elders. The negative reports regarding youth have been widely reported over the years. Look at these comments through the ages:

> A young man is a sort of puppy who only plays with an argument; and is reasoned into and out of his opinions every day; he soon begins to believe nothing, and brings himself and philosophy into discredit.
> —Plato, *The Republic*, Book 7

> [Young people] have exalted notions, because they have not yet been humbled by life or learnt its necessary limitations; moreover, their hopeful disposition makes them think themselves equal to great things...All their mistakes are in the direction of doing things excessively and vehemently. They disobey Chilon's precept by overdoing everything, they love too much and hate too much, and the same thing with everything else. They think they know everything, and

are always quite sure about it; this, in fact, is why they overdo everything.   —Aristotle, *Rhetoric*, Book II, Chapter 12

Youth were never more sawcie, yea never more savagely sawcie, and
people never more lawlesse: the Ancient are scorned, the honourable
are condemned, the Magistrate is not dreaded.
                                    —Rev. Thomas Barnes, *The Wise-Mans Forecast Against*
                                                              The Evill Time, 1624

It affords a very gloomy prospect to see so many young persons who
were the hope of their parents, & might have been the ornaments &
pillars of their country, sink into vice & sensuality, lost, not only to a
sense of virtue, but of common modesty & decency, giving themselves
up to the foulest blasphemies, defying the God that made them, with
oaths and curses abusing the hand which feeds them, sporting themselves with the name of the everlasting God & continually invoking
the thunderbolt of wrath upon their guilty heads!
                                    —*Diary of Enos Hitchcock*, 1899

What an interesting historical review of youth through the years. Our language
has changed but the concepts remain the same: youth are felt to be impetuous,
rebellious, and not be trusted with earthly responsibilities or the things of God.

It is not easy to predict the future, but the more data and information we have,
the easier it becomes. Looking at the history of youth ministry in America can
help. Here's a quick review of where we've been and where we are now:

- The Sunday School era (1790s)

- Early para-church movements (1820s through 1950s)

- Student volunteer movement on college campuses (1860s through 1900)

- Billy Graham crusades (1930s through 1990s)

- Jesus Movement (1960s and 1970s)

- Interdenominational and mega-church movements (1980s through
  2000s)

- Social or information era (2005 through the present)

I grew up in a youth ministry in the 1970s that basically included acoustic worship, my youth pastor preaching or teaching us, and a prayer time at the close of the service. Much of youth ministry was done this way. However, there was also a major emphasis on small groups in the Sunday school setting. Who could forget their Sunday school days with other seventh-graders in the musty old basement classroom that was hot in the summer and cold in the winter?!

The philosophy of youth ministry today in the twenty-first century is altogether different. Generally, there are many styles and kinds of youth ministries in America, but most are all about programming and culture-building. A look around the country will find that most of youth ministry is personality driven, has a unique name, includes food or snacks, spends time playing activities such as games, and is highly entertaining and attractive. Theology is all but missing in the general youth ministry setting.

THE EMPHASIS IN GEN Z YOUTH MINISTRY HAS BEEN PLACED ON ME-OLOGY AND PERSONALITY RATHER THAN THEOLOGY AND DISCIPLESHIP.

This is a far cry from the classic model of youth ministry. Really, Gen Z youth ministry has become program-based and industry-minded. The emphasis has been placed on *me-ology* and personality rather than *theology* and discipleship.

So, with that quick review in mind, here are five futurist ethics that I believe must be a part of youth ministry in the next ten years, if the Lord tarries.

FIVE ETHICS AND SPIRITUAL DISCIPLINES FOR THE FUTURE OF YOUTH MINISTRY

1. CONTEXTUAL OR MISSIOLOGY ETHIC

It is important to understand the relationship between *sociology* and *theology*. They go hand in hand as context (sociology) and content (theology).

We must raise students who want to *be* the church and not just *go* to church. We must get students to understand that they can serve God in the context of their world, to help them see that worship, prayer, and reading their Bible does not just take place at youth group once a week. They need to live out their faith in the family, the school, their teams, and in the places where they hang out.

A missional mindset of every youth leader must be present in neutral site settings of students and teenagers. Youth leaders must be seen at each of the places where teenagers do life. When a student understands that their faith does not have an address on the church property, they will have grasped one of the most important principles of youth ministry—that God is present in all things in and outside of the church building!

Here are some practical ways to bring missiology to youth ministry:

- Create youth ministry events that are not held at the church
- Move the youth ministry to a high school or community setting quarterly
- Use the language of the youth culture in your messaging
- Take advantage of social media to bring the gospel footprint into culture
- Teach a strong apologetic or biblical mission to students so they understand their place in the world

2. DIVERSITY ETHIC

The latest research states that 51 percent of Gen Z is non-white, the largest percentage in American history. This fact must shape the way we do youth ministry in the next ten years as we look at language, the diversity of the youth team, race education, and total inclusion.

Do you know that we could be on the verge of rewriting the race relations narrative in the church and ultimately the culture? We could leave a story of healing for Alpha Gen if we simply continue with this unity, healing, and inclusive emphasis in youth ministry. By doing this, we will have a hand in the makeover of our nation in just a decade. The research is clear and undeniable. Now we need a clear vision and trends to support it.

What does that look like?

- A diversity make-up of the leadership team that places value at the authority level

- The language that we use in our messaging must be current and reflect race relations

- Involvement of every student in leadership positions

- Race-inclusive strategies for social media posting

3. FAMILY ETHIC

The family has disintegrated in America. We're not just raising a fatherless generation anymore. We are raising a fatherless, a motherless, and a sibling-less generation. The classic family structure that was such a strength in our nation's past has been lost. But youth ministry has the potential to change society at the family level. The fundamental principle that brings change to any society begins at home. So, youth ministry must model a family ethic if we are going to impact young people today. Here are a few practical ways to do that:

- Modeling affection in the youth ministry setting brings security to teenagers and closes the door on predators who are preying on our children

- Promoting the value of brotherly and sisterly relationships within the youth ministry brings accountability to children and protection to the group

- Making sure the youth leadership team is multigenerational and mirrors the family makeup in order to reflect a healthy society

- Providing parental training sessions annually in the youth ministry creates a revolutionary and value-add to the validity of youth ministry in the church

Many people blame government, education, social media, entertainment and the arts, and a multitude of other things for the condition of our society, but the number one issue is the health of the family. Youth ministry must get this right. If we do not, we raise another weakened generation.

4. THE SEXUALITY ETHIC

Identity among the Gen Z and Alpha Gen sets is confusing at best. I say this because there has been so much redefinition going on as it relates to gender.

I LAST COUNTED OVER FIFTY GENDER TYPE NAMES THAT HAVE BEEN CREATED JUST IN THE PAST TWO OR THREE YEARS. IT IS STUNNING TO SEE THE VARIETY OF WAYS THAT PEOPLE DEFINE THEIR SEXUALITY.

If youth ministry is going to have a voice in this latest sexual revolution, we must define a biblical identity for teenagers today. They cannot get their identity from culture. Yet this ethic is not just about identity. It is about purity and the restoration and redemption of anyone.

Here are some practical steps to protect the principle of the sanctity of sexuality and gender:

- Inform students of the theology of sexuality and gender
- Discuss identity in youth ministry in order to reset the concept in Scripture
- Organize parent meetings to educate the family on current social trends and language
- Do not be afraid to talk about issues that are seen as *hands off*
- Hold annual seminars with professionals to help train the church

Each of these ethics are critical to the future of youth ministry. However, the greatest future principle or ethic in youth ministry is the valuation of theology and spiritual formation. When the ethic of theology is restored to youth ministry, we will raise a generation who has everything they need to handle each of these first four needed ethics.

5. THEOLOGY ETHIC

Discipleship must be restored in youth ministry, or we will raise another generation void of a biblical worldview. Another Gen Z trait we have shared in this work that should influence the future of youth ministry is that only 4 percent of this generation has a biblical worldview. And this generation includes more atheists than any other generation in American history. This is not an encouraging trend. We must see a renewed emphasis on theology in youth ministry.

A theology ethic is critical for youth ministry in the future because of the generational loss of theology in Gen Z. All of the research statistics show a spiral downward in youth Christian thinking and worldview. The research has shown that Gen Z is dangerously God-less. Even among Christian teenagers who attend youth group, only one-third can name half of the Ten Commandments. These startling statistics demonstrate how critical it is for youth ministry to place theology at the center of our work.

Here's how we can do that:

- A greater emphasis on preaching directly from the Bible and not a movie series, headline news, or social media
- Creation of a preaching or teaching series around a passage of the Scriptures for an entire month
- More application and practical teaching from the Bible placed in the context of our teenagers' lives
- Biblical worship
- Biblical counseling
- Redeeming social media for the purpose of theology

The need for each of these ethics in youth ministry cannot be understated.

FINALLY

As we have noted, we have a crisis in this generation—we are serving a God we do not know.

All the research statistics show that the theology in this generation is anemic. However, if we are not careful, the Alpha Generation to follow is going to be even worse off than Gen Z.

Each of these disciplines in this book or the ethics of this conclusion will help to shape what youth ministry looks like in the coming years. It will require all of us doing our part. Hopefully, within these pages, you will find the theoretical and the practical guidelines to disciple your own life, the youth ministry you direct, or, if you are a parent, your own children.

We cannot deny the future impact of youth ministry on our culture. Some of our nation's next great politicians, educators, business leaders, entertainers, service professionals, and spiritual leaders are growing up right now in the church. This reality should motivate current youth leadership to shape a different outcome than what we have seen in the last two decades.

One thing is very clear: whatever we have been doing in youth ministry over the last twenty years is not working. A prophetic look at the future of youth ministry will help its leaders stay current in the field. Without a doubt, the future of youth ministry must include the development of *Next Gen Faith*.

ABOUT THE AUTHOR

After four decades of youth leadership in the church, parachurch, and university setting, Jeff Grenell founded ythology to inspire, educate, and resource youth leaders to prepare the next generation to lead in the church and the world

Jeff is also the Next Gen Specialist at North Central University in Minneapolis, Minnesota, where he and his wife Jessica are Directors of the Institute for Next Gen (iNG), a youth education, training, and resource center for developing Next Gen leaders globally.

A former youth pastor at churches in Michigan, Indiana, and Ohio, Jeff attended Evangel University in Springfield, Missouri, where he received his B.A. in Communications and Theology and his M.A. in Organizational Leadership.

Jeff and Jessica have six children and six grandchildren and reside in Minneapolis.

Jeff can be reached at www.ythology.com or on multiple social media platforms for events, leadership development, resources, anti-sex-trafficking, humanitarian aid, and educational leadership.

For more on North Central University's Institute for Next Gen, visit www.northcentral.edu/ing.

BIBLIOGRAPHY

Barna, George, *American Worldview Inventory 2021-22: The Annual Report on the State of Worldview in the United States* (Glendale, AZ: Arizona Christian University Press, 2021).

Barna, George, *Revolution* (Carol Stream, IL: Tyndale House Publishers, 2006).

Barna Group, *Gen Z: The Culture, Beliefs and Motivations Shaping the Next Generation* (Ventura, CA: Barna Publishing, 2018 and 2021).

Bethune, Sophie, "Stress in America 2022: Concerned for the future, beset by inflation," American Psychological Association, October 2022; www.apa.org/news/press/releases/stress/2022/concerned-future-inflation.

Brother Lawrence, *The Practice of the Presence of God* (New Kensington, PA: Whitaker House, 1982).

Brown, Stuart, "Play is more than just fun," TED talk, March 12, 2009; www.ted.com/talks/stuart_brown_play_is_more_than_just_fun.

Chan, Francis, *Forgotten God: Reversing Our Tragic Neglect of the Holy Spirit* (Colorado Springs, CO: David C. Cook Publishing, 2009).

Collins, Jim, *Good to Great: Why Some Companies Make the Leap and Others Don't* (New York: HarperCollins, 2001).

FEED Research, Pompano Beach, Florida; feed.bible/research.

Graham, Billy, "My Heart Breaks for America," July 19, 2012; billygraham.org/story/billy-graham-my-heart-aches-for-america.

Green, Kai, "Still Shining On! Remembering John Lennon With 65 of His Most Famous and Profound Quotes," *Parade* magazine newsletter, November 25, 2021; parade.com/1299046/kaigreen/john-lennon-quotes.

Halsey Jr., Ashley, "Ending the Mystery of the 'Rules,'" *The American Rifleman*, January 1973, vol. 121 no. 1, regarding "How to Destroy the West" by Vladimir Lenin, reprinted in *Life Lines*, February 12, 1973, vol. 15 no. 17; www.jstor.org/stable/community.28146662#metadata_info_tab_contents.

Hartig, Hannah, "Americans broadly negative about the state of the nation, but most see a better year ahead," Pew Research Center, January 25, 2022; www.pewresearch.org/fact-tank/2022/01/25/americans-broadly-negative-about-the-state-of-the-nation-but-most-see-a-better-year-ahead.

Lenin, Vladimir, *Lenin: Selected Works* (Moscow: Progress Publishers, 1970).

Noebel, David, *Understanding the Times* (Eugene, OR: Harvest House Publishers, 1994).

Pratney, W.A., *The Nature and Character of God* (Ada, MI: Bethany House, 1988).

"Speed Up Drive for Total Disarmament of Civilians," *Common Sense*, January 15, 1964, Issue No. 421, quoting *New World News*, February 1946; www.jstor.org/stable/community.28144632?seq=1#metadata_info_tab_contents.